NO MORE chains

SUCCEEDING AGAINST THE ODDS

She EO
Publishing

NO MORE CHAINS

11 Stories of Chain Breaking Transformations That Will Set YOU Free

11 *FREE* Gifts Inside Just For You

- Success kits to help you pull back the mental barriers that prevent love, peace and abundance from coming into your life.
- Assessments to analyze if you are ready to move to a new level in life.
- Guides on becoming more productive and how to reach a level of success by bringing awareness to your distractions so that you can avoid them.
- Parenting tips on breaking generational chains.
- A 31 day devotional full of scriptures, prayers, and affirmations to assist women living with a diagnosis in truly manifesting their God ordained healing, and deliverance intended uniquely for them.
- PLUS SO MANY MORE!

Empowered By R. Ari Squires

Get your copy of the NO MORE CHAINS Documentary and
see these transformative stories come to life.

www.NoMoreChainsFilm.com

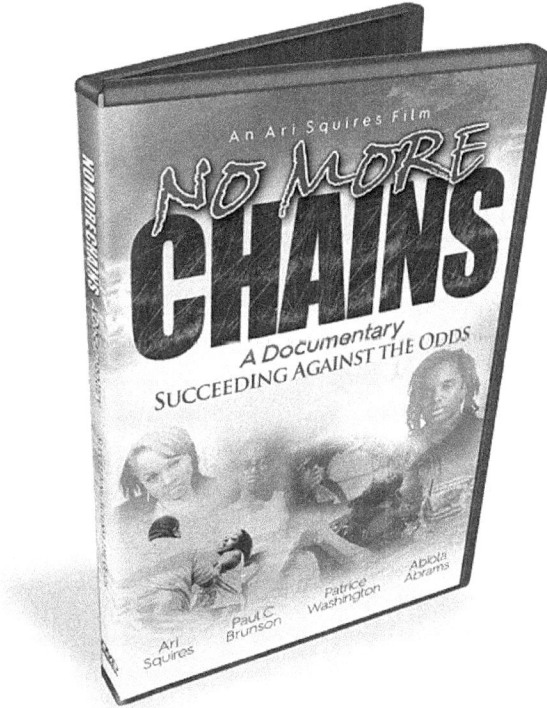

Cover Design: Jasper White EOS Media Group www.mediaemg.com. Interior Design: SheEO Publishing

ISBN-13: 978-0692967843

ISBN-10: 0692967842

For general information or other products and services, contact Ari Squires at www.AriSquires.com, info@arisquires.com

Published in the United States by
SheEO Publishing Company
526 Wolfe Street
Suite 1
Fredericksburg, VA 22401
www.SheEOPublishing.com

Printed in the United States of America

This book is dedicated to and in the memory of the fearless Harriet Tubman who said, *"I freed a thousand slaves. I could have freed a thousand more if only they knew they were slaves."*

Harriet Tubman was born a slave, but she never, not once cultivated the mentality of a slave. She is the prime example of succeeding against the odds and taking those who comprehended her vision with her.

We dedicate this book to her and all the women like her, whose endeavors are to *free* others from their chains.

Women are taking the world by storm by breaking glass ceilings, dominating in our industries, and being change agents while not making any apologies.

Keep striving for excellence and continue to push. Our work is not done yet but together we will impact the world!

ABOUT ARI SQUIRES

Ari Squires is a success coach using her soul-based mindset mastery and unique business success approach to help women who are in transition create the lives and businesses that they love.

Ari, SheEO of Aspire with Ari Professional Coaching & Seminars is on a heart-filled mission to empower women, teens and entrepreneurs to do what they love and live their best life. She is an author, success coach and an advocate for youth leadership, who empowers people all over the country to move beyond their fears, get clear on what they truly want and carve out a life they love.

Ari knows the struggle of being unhappy and wanting more. Due to this unease and feeling the pull of wanting to create her own life instead of settling for what someone handed to her, she courageously opened a Dance & Performing Arts School to fill a void in her community of helping girls build confidence. She quickly built her brand in no time by what she titles "consistency": Consistency in branding, marketing and live event promotions.

Ari's unique style of branding and positioning put her and her business on the map and generated six figures in revenue within its first year and beyond.

Today, as a Success Coach, Ari assists her clients in identifying what they truly want in their lives and businesses. She takes a strengths based approach to help women own and grow in their greatness, focusing on each client's unique "gifts" to help them understand what is and isn't lining up with those gifts, then teaches them how to train themselves to attract abundance and wealth into their lives.

Having formally lived on hard times, incarceration and homelessness, Ari developed a mindset that even through the toughest storms, you must still see the rainbow. Because of her past, Ari has dedicated her life to helping and empowering a growing number of people get out of their comfort zones, tap into their glorious gifts and release the chains from the prison of their minds, so that they take control, and become the CEO's of their lives and not the employees to their circumstances, and make massive strides towards their dreams to profit abundantly in life and business.

Some of her clients include CVS Pharmacy, Mary Washington Hospital, Spotsylvania County Schools, Chicago City Public Schools, and several sororities and local youth organizations; she has also appeared on various TV and radio media outlets sharing her expertise.

Other Books By Ari Squires

Release The Chains – A Woman's Roadmap for Finding the Strength to Reclaim Her Destiny

All I See Is Possibility – Wisdom & Inspiration on Getting What YOU Want

The Mindset of a She.E.O. – 7 Core Principles of Sustaining Success as a Woman in Business

What They Are Saying About Ari Squires

Working with Ari Squires over the last year has completely changed both my personal and my professional life. When I first started working with Ari, I had no clue about how to run a business or how to be a successful entrepreneur so I knew that this journey would be a rough one for me but I was willing to learn. I sat down with Ari just wanting to be a good makeup artist but after working with her for almost a year, I now have more clarity on the endless possibilities that exist in my business of being not only an amazing makeup artist but a beauty educator and a coach. I went from having zero customers at first to being completely booked up through the spring and summer. With the help of her amazing coaching services and Mastermind group, I am now able to have multiple revenue sources through my business, increased clientele, an endless network of business professionals, and the confidence and know-how to make my business a six figure business. This experience has been life-changing to say the least and I'm beyond grateful for this journey.

Shavon Dotson, Owner & Founder
Flawless Faces www.flawlessfacesmua.com

~~~~~~~~~~~~~~~~~~~~~

I conducted my first education seminar under the guidance and assistance of my success coach Ari Squires where she also served as the Keynote Speaker with her signature presentation, *A Polished Presence*. As she expounded on the importance of soft skills in the salon profession, you can see that she had everyone's attention and the entire room was engaged. Needless to say the event was a resounding success.

In spite of this and partly due to my disability I fell back into a rut. I did not use that momentum to catapult my venture. Self-doubt and negative self-talk practically threw me into a bout with depression that laid me up for days at a time. I was barely functioning.

It was on one of those days God and the Universe conspired to use Ari as the conduit the amber to reignite the passion and desire I have for the hair business through a simple message of encouragement...

Hey Niambi,
I didn't want anything. Just checking on you? How are you? Have you made any new efforts to continue with the classes? They were such a great idea and much needed and obviously well received. Don't give up on them.
I look forward to hearing from you soon.
Happy Holidays!

Sincerely,
Ari Squires

She was unaware of my mental state as we hadn't spoken in months. Her encouragement sparked the flame to believe in myself and to take a second look. And eyes have not seen, ears have not heard all the amazing things that have happened just two weeks later. We closed on our new home, I'm hosting a mega conference with a leading and in high demand salon educator under Ari's guidance once again, and I began the process of building a new salon.
Ari is the Truth being used by God to share her gifts with women in business.
Niambi Rockcliffe
BEST by Niambi

~~~~~~~~~~~~~~~~~~~~~

Clarity. Determination. Focus. These are just a few words to describe my outcome since working with Ari. I always knew there was something more for me, but yet could not figure out how to accomplish my dreams. Through intense coaching and mentoring, I have been able to write a book, host workshops and live "On Purpose". My life has been transformed by the endless possibilities. Thank you Ari for believing in me and pushing me into greatness.
Leslie Y. Jackson
Author. Speaker. Vision Strategist.
www.leslieyjackson.com

~~~~~~~~~~~~~~~~~~~~~

Like many, I thought about coaching but I didn't want another monthly bill. I met Ari at a small women's conference in Dinwiddie, VA one summer. Once Ari shared her story I realized we had similar backgrounds so I knew I wanted her to coach me. Before coaching with Ari, I used to tell people I had a Jump Rope Business, but now when asked, "What do you do?" I'm able to confidently say "I use the exciting sport of double-dutch to build confidence, improve cardiovascular health and nutrition, while empowering youth to set and reach goals." I began coaching in September 2015 and at that time I was doing short 4 week sessions with small organizations. As of May 15, 2016, I can proudly say that JumpStarz has current contracts and/or has provided services for the County of Henrico Recreation, County of Prince George, City of Richmond Parks & Recreation and the County of Chesterfield, American Family Fitness and Fort Lee Military base.

I am happy I decided to invest in me! I actually calculated my March invoices and noticed it was greater than my total coaching fee.

Patricia Clement, Founder
JumpStarz www.thejumpstarz.com

~~~~~~~~~~~~~~~~~~~~~

I have had the pleasure of participating in the P.U.S.H. Mastermind Group powered by Ari Squires. This was my first professional dealings with Mrs. Squires, and to my surprise, she over-delivered on the expectations she set for the group. WOW!!! Ari has done an outstanding job of creating such an unmatched synergy amongst the group, which consisted of ladies from many different backgrounds, and professional experiences. I am beyond pleased with her knowledge and professionalism, and am further along in my coaching practice than what I was when I began this mastermind journey; this speaks volumes toward Ari's credibility because we are only four sessions in to this experience. At this rate, I can only imagine where I'll be once we're done. Ari's knowledge, paired with her dedication and willingness to serve others makes her the ideal choice for anyone   seeking a reputable, results-producing business coach.

Keisha M. Green, CEO, MBA, CPC
Certified Personal Development Coach

~~~~~~~~~~~~~~~~~~~~~

Working with Ari as my business coach has been a great life changing, chain releasing experience. She helped me to declutter my thoughts and identify how I can serve others with my gift. I would recommend Ari as a success coach as she has tried and true experience in overcoming obstacles and motivating others to realize their true potential.

Ebony Moss
Personal Accountability & Fitness Professional

~~~~~~~~~~~~~~~~~~~~~~

Ari Squires is another one of God's Blessings in Life. She came to me (I found her) at a time when I needed that extra push and encouragement, knowledge and know how on ways to build the business of my dreams. In her P.U.S.H. Mastermind Class she gives the blueprint step by step of being successful in business/life.

Tinika Jackson-Herndon
Owner of Soulkisses 365 Boutique by Tinika
www.sk365boutique.com

Table of Contents

Foreword

It is such an honor to introduce the following book. The stories within are so raw, so vulnerable, so powerful, and so courageous. It takes courage for a woman to expose her hidden, inner self to her most intimate friends, yet to display that hidden self to an anonymous and unnumbered audience takes strength beyond words.

If there is one thing these women are sure to have, it's strength. They have the strength to not only endure the situations they've found themselves in but to overcome those battles, to break through, and prevail. Emotional and physical abuse at the hands of their parents or loved ones could not diminish the light that shines in these women. Patterns of neglect and abandonment could not hold them down. Each and every one discovered the powerful light within themselves and broke free of the chains that would have destroyed them.

We know that there is strength in numbers. This book reveals the truth of that phrase. Alone, these women were brave, but together they are unstoppable. Leading them is Ari Squires—business coach, speaker, and transformational filmmaker. She is a living demonstration of how far one person can go once they become determined to break their chains. Once homeless and imprisoned, Ari found her light and changed her life. She now shines that light on those who attend her life-changing workshops, programs, and coaching sessions.

Her newest life-changing event is the No More Chains Movement. A book, a song, and soon a film, the No More Chains Movement inspires women and men from all walks of life to break free of the things that are holding them back and dimming their inner light. Whether it comes from abuse, drugs, illness, or finances, Ari and the women in this book know there is no such thing as a chain that cannot be broken. This book will help you unearth your own chain and show you how to break free.

No More Chains goes above and beyond the average book anthology. Ari has used her experience and expertise to provide tools and strategies to aid you on your journey. The reflections and exercises within will set you on the path toward freedom. With Ari and the 11 authors on your side, you'll see yourself making discoveries, having revelations, setting goals, and making plans. They will help you find your inner light.

I encourage you to look at these women as proof of how much strength may be lying within you and as inspiration for moving steadfastly in your life. After finishing *No More Chains*, I know you will find the strength to see that there is nothing holding you back from being who you desire to be. So, read the stories, ask yourself the questions, find your chain, and join the movement.

Let *No More Chains* be more than a book. Let it be a lifestyle.

Darrin Dewitt Henson

Actor, Author, "Ain't That The Truth"

Introduction

Hello, my sisters and brothers. I welcome you to the ***No More Chains Movement.*** Let me inform you right now that you are about to be taken on a journey that will force you to think about your life, goals and purpose - and begin to plan further for the legacy you wish to leave, and be a part of.

Make sure that you read every single story and sit in silence with the message, and think about how what you've read relates to your own life. It may not be the same story, but trust and believe that there will be similar chains. I would like for you to get centered, reflect, read, cry, shout - whatever you have to do - as you put yourself in the shoes of these women, as they pour their hearts out, boldly and courageously releasing their chains.

My mission in life is to help people remove themselves from their stories, from their pain and their shame. It's time to start standing in front of our stories instead of behind them. We can no longer let what happened to us in our past define who we are today, tomorrow, and in our future. We have to stand in front of it without being victims. Being a victim only suppresses our psychological, emotional and financial freedom.

I created the No More Chains book anthology because I wanted this to be not just a movement of sharing these wonderful and glorious stories, but I wanted to provide a resource where you can gain knowledge, get success tools and life-enhancing strategies. I also want you to use this as a journal, something you can write in and come back to, and check your progress. We can read all day long, but until we actually write things down and take action, we will never see results. If we do not act, we will always be wrapped in chains. We will always be held captive by our own narratives.

As you go through this book, pull out a pen and write. I ask you specific goal-planning questions. From here, you start with a plan for your chain release. You can't have a plan without a date, so you will see as you go through this book, there will be specific questions to help you release your chains.

We all have chains. The only way to release your chains and move into a space of no more chains is to be authentic, to be transparent, and to be real and honest with yourself and admit that, *there are some things that are keeping me stuck. There are some things that are holding me back. There are some things that I need to release so I can make room for the new, and so I can make room for what the universe has for me.* But you can't do that unless you are willing to be vulnerable, just like every single woman in this book has been. Your vulnerability will take you to abundance in life and business.

Every single one of these women has shared things about themselves that they haven't told many, and now they are free. They are living free. They have no more chains. Now they can be all that they want to be, and they passionately want the same for you.

Enjoy these stories, but remember: change only begins when *you* do the work.

Generational Chains Broken

Artwork unknown

I grew up like a neglected weed - ignorant of liberty, having no experience of it.

~Harriet Tubman

About Q. Futrell

Quniana Futrell, known as "Author Q", is an advocate for change! A trainer, author and speaker, she works with key groups critical to rebuilding families affected by incarceration. This mission was born from personal experience.

Author Q was once broken, navigating a childhood with both parents incarcerated.

Now a wife and mom, she also loves to help other moms, who look well put together but are broken on the inside, change their story!

Keeping momentum as a change-agent for families, Author Q released her first children's book, *Our Moms*, in November 2015. *Our Moms* is a conversation-starter for parents, professionals, or service providers who live or work with children of incarcerated parents.

Proficient in curriculum development, Author Q created a program for incarcerated parents and administers the course weekly, at a jail in Suffolk, VA.

Author Q also hosts seminars nationally for teachers to gain confidence, support and resources to effectively reach the children of incarcerated parents in their classrooms. Her approach also teaches educators how to support the children's families. She aims to live in a world where healthy parents and teachers work together to produce healthy children.

Author Q has been featured in multiple media outlets for her work in the community. This proven Children's Champion motto is: Change the Family, Change the World!

Chapter 1

1 in 14

Q. FUTRELL

-oooooooo-

1 of every 14 children have a parent who is incarcerated.

The great Langston Hughes said it best in his famous poem called, *Mother to Son* when he wrote, "Life for me ain't been no crystal stair." Relating that to my life, I grew up in Newark, NJ. Being from "Brick City" has afforded me many good, bad and horrific experiences. Both of my parents were in and out of local jails and state prisons. My parents were never together, so I didn't have the experience of growing up in a two-biological-parent household. They both loved, and I do mean LOVED, the opposite sex.

As if that wasn't enough, my parents were also addicted to various drugs. My mom more so than my dad which made things worse because she was my custodial parent. My mother had friends that entertained her addictions so I was always over strangers' homes and even would spend the night at their homes simply because they had children also. Being passed around from house to house and relative to relative left the door wide open for sexual abuse.

My mother had other things to do. I would come home to an empty house limited to no food. I didn't know it at the time that a syrup or mayonnaise sandwich wasn't a real thing but it was all that I had.

Now, when you have parents who are addicted to anything, it is often hard to know how you will be treated at any given moment if they have not had their "fix." Often times, the smallest things can soar into something grand. I will never forget the time I allowed my cousin to wear my mom's outfit home. I knew she would get it back so I didn't think she would mind; OHHHH, which was not the case. I don't think I remember another time in my life EVER being beaten so badly. My mother whipped me with anything she could put her hands on at the time. I will never forget her holding a vacuum cord and saying, "I will crucify you like Jesus Christ if don't get my stuff back!"

As if that wasn't enough, before the whipping began, she told me to call my cousin to get her clothes back and that is what I did. I had the phone to my ear and they didn't answer so I left a message. While leaving the message right in the middle of my sentence, the first strike came...the bulk of this horrific experience was recorded on my cousin's house phone. The worst part of this whole experience wasn't the fact that I couldn't believe my mother physically abused me and it wasn't even the threats of what she would do to me if I didn't return her outfit. The worst of it all was that my grandmother sat there and watched the whole thing. She just sat there consoling my other cousin while he cried and simply told me right after, "you can't let people wear your mom's stuff!"

There are many chains I have released given the variety of experiences to which I was exposed, but for the sake of my one chapter I will say this: I have released the chain of becoming what hurt me the most, my parents! I made the decision to not simply sit in my pain and allow it to leave me negative, bitter and suicidal, but rather an overcomer and more than a conqueror!

Succeeding Against the Odds

Research says 75% or more of children who were abused turn to become abusers themselves. Although we learn that a vast majority do not become abusers, too many do.

I am grateful to have succeeded against the odds. All odds were stacked against me. I could have easily become who and what hurt me. Now, looking at where I am today, I wouldn't consider myself to have "made it" yet, but I have certainly succeeded.

Honestly, I could have easily ended up dead by now! I could be selling my body going from bed to bed searching for love. I could be somewhere with a needle in my arm struggling with an overdose. I could be in prison and be a convicted felon.

When I say, "I succeeded against the odds," it isn't a boastful thing. It is me saying, "I know the society bet against me," but somewhere in my personal card game of War, war was declared on me, and this time I had the higher card!

The late Maya Angelou couldn't have said it any better, STILL, I RISE! I rose against adversity, I rose against the lack of parental love; I rose against abuse, and against drug addiction...STILL, I RISE and have succeeded against the odds.

Certainly, simply telling you I succeeded, but not showing you how you too can succeed would be pointless.

Moving Past the Pain

Moving past the pain is certainly not something that came easy. It wasn't until I learned how to forgive and why I needed to forgive in order for me to move past the hurt. It was at an altar call at my church that the Lord gave me the cure of forgiveness. I had to forgive my parents for all that had happened because they did the best they knew *how* to do. See that to me was profound. I had to take a step back and ask myself "who raised them and how was that relationship?"

What I never understood was that, they both had a story. They both had endured some of the many things that were passed on to me. I then learned it was generational. After forgiving them, I then learned that I had to have boundaries with them in order to truly walk in peace. Now, I own who they are, what they did, how they treated me and I LOVE them anyway! Why? Because *everyone* deserves GRACE! Does it give them a pass...absolutely not! However, it does allow me the opportunity to have a relationship with them and my children by my terms and my way.

The Chains Released

This experience has changed me for the better. I am the woman, mother, and friend I am today because of my parents. I worship and trust God the way I do because of them. I firmly believe that ALL things have worked together for my good! I know that had it not been for my traumatic experiences, I would not be able to help another child who endures currently the same thing. I am transparent in my walk knowing that my life's stories will birth hope to a hopeless generation. I have allowed my pain to now be my purpose! Although I have been detoured quite a bit on my journey, I am confident in knowing that ALL that God started in me, he will complete!

Now standing tall, I walk on water daily. I don't know how it's all going to work out but I believe that it will. I own my weaknesses and am grateful for my strengths.

The late Rita Pierson, a well-known educator, said, "*Every* child deserves a champion! An adult who will never give up on them, who understands the power of connection, and insists they become the very best they can possibly be!" I have coined myself as the "Children's Champion!" I shape and change the world by healing the inner broken child that resides in adults. I work with adults who live or work with children who are broken and need support. It is because of all I have endured that has created a relentless drive for me to pursue this journey unapologetically! I won't apologize for what I have today. No one ever apologized to me for the pain. I stand tall as their champion of change and curse breaker. IT IS TIME! I had to become my own rescue and so do you! Release the Chains, Live on Purpose and Go Back to Rescue Others! My motto for life is Change the Family, Change the World.

Here is the Lesson

I want you to focus on this short story shared with me by a friend: Imagine sitting in your chair reading this book and I come behind you and pull the chair from underneath you. Whose fault would it be that you are on the floor? Mine, right?

Now let's imagine I come back in two weeks and you are still on the floor...whose fault is it now that you are still on the floor?

The blame is now NOT me! It is YOUR fault that you spent so much time on the floor. Sadly, for most of you, your two years have become 20-30 years. For years I too was on the floor waiting for someone to extend a hand to help me but it never came. I eventually had to get up on my own and GET OFF THE FLOOR!

The lesson I need you to catch is this: although the pain is real, it will pass. Be relentless in your journey knowing that the life you want is at your fingertips. Surround yourself with positive and motivating people and *all* good things will happen for you. Don't believe the hype. You are not alone. There are plenty of women who have been raped, molested; on drugs; a drunk; and so much worse, but guess what? They survived! Here is the good news, SO WILL YOU! Don't Quit!

Are you ready to take the leap into your greatness? I hope you are because let me tell you a secret...you will never be fully ready which is why you just have to leap. Remember success isn't about how you feel, it's about your faith or belief in yourself that you *can* do this! I want to help you with this. I help mothers who are well put together on the outside, but broken on the inside to change their story.

Since I was broken and raised by two previously incarcerated parents, I also work with families and organizations that live or work with a child that has a parent incarcerated. I work in the jails, prisons, schools, and any business that welcomes me to speak out on this topic. I have developed a book called, *Our Moms*. This interactive book engages the sensitive conversation of parental incarceration. This is not your typical book; it has started a 1 in 14 movement.

You have to release your chain because you have something on the inside of you that can truly impact this world for generations. YOU are GREAT! YOU are powerful beyond measure. Do you really know how great you can be if you release it?

Guess what? I want to help you with that. I want to help you get through this with genuine support. I don't want anything in return from you. I have a 3-day video series called, "Parenting with Confidence" that I created with you in mind.

In just 3 days, I take you on a journey from past, present to future! If you have ever said:

1. "Well, I wasn't taught that."
2. "My family has been doing it like this for years so now I do too."
3. This course is for you!
4. If you were raised by parents who did the best they could but left you with many uncertainties as a parent, THIS COURSE IS FOR YOU! Go to www.bit.ly/pwc3day and get your free gift.

As a thank you for taking the three-day #PWC challenge, you will be invited to join my elite tribe of Champions who are determined to Parent with Confidence. We are a bunch of women and some men who can honestly say, "Although I wasn't taught how to parent, I will parent my children with confidence!"

Learn more about me and follow my movement! Join me in changing the narrative for children across this country! Follow me on social media @AuthorQFutrell on Periscope, Facebook, Snapchat, Twitter and Instagram. If you are in Metro Atlanta, join me every Thursday at 5pm EST on 99.1 FM for my Talk Radio Show, "Change the Family, Change the World."

A Word of Change

If you continue to hang around foolish people and do foolish things, your life will become a joke! - Author Q

Without a shadow of doubt, YOU are a Champion! I want your family strengthened and healthy! If *we* can Change the Family, *we* can Change the World!

No More Stagnation:

This is a powerful story of not allowing your past to define your future. As you will see, the common theme throughout this section is generational ailments that could have kept the author stuck. But with courage, grace and strong faith, Q did not become a statistic. She did not become what she could have been.

Are you following a curse passed down from generation to generation? Are you fearful of something due to something that happened in your life?

> *I want you to break this curse, today. Right now, so that your children and their children do not have to live their lives in fear or stagnation. You have the power to change your story.* ~Ari Squires

What are you doing right now in your life that you realize has been passed down to you?

_____

_____

_____

_____

_____

When exactly will you release that chain and how? Write your new story below.

_____

_____

_____

_____

_____

About Taliah Shiree Graves

Taliah Shiree Graves is a motivational blogger, humble life and wellness mentor, accountability coach and speaker.

Through her God-given gift of connecting with people, she has dedicated her life's work to providing genuine guidance and a listening ear to help women going through transitional seasons in their lives.

With more than 10 years of mentoring experience and bringing out the best and most positive parts of women, she motivates and uplifts in a way that shows them love, builds them up, and brings out the very best in them. She helps them dig deeper and become more aware of themselves. As a result, she helps them find peace and healing in their lives so that they stop making the same mistakes.

Countless women are saying nothing but great things about Taliah and how she "listens from within and not from other people's perspectives," how she's "able to empathize and understand what others have gone through," and that she is "genuine and not just an act."

Chapter 2

Who Am I Truly Living For?

TALIAH SHIREE GRAVES

—◦◦◦◦◦◦◦—

"The two most important days in your life are the day you were born and the day you find out why." ~Mark Twain

It took me 27 years to discover me. To discover why I was born. To dig deep and be unapologetic about who I was and rest with clarity about it all. During my 27th year of life, a huge shift occurred, and I have not been the same since.

I'm a firm believer that the underlying reason a lot of us lack peace in our lives is that we don't have a clear plan. It was certainly the reason I lived uneasy and anxious for so long. However, I soon found that I couldn't create a plan without understanding what my purpose was.

It's almost impossible to devise and enact a sound plan for your life if you are unclear about your purpose. And in order to discover your purpose, you need a clear idea of who you are, what your boundaries are, where you aren't willing to settle; and you must trust yourself. When you have these things figured out, you're in a better position to discover peace, live your best life, and operate as the best version of yourself.

Humble thought: Our purpose helps establish the GPS for our lives. We all feel more comfortable and secure when we have a GPS directing us where we are trying to go, so why wouldn't you want to discover it for yourself and live it?

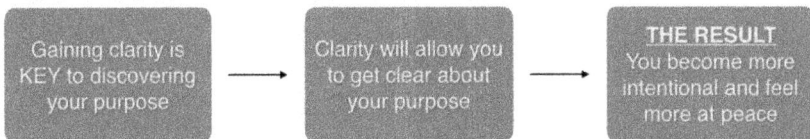

| Gaining clarity is KEY to discovering your purpose | → | Clarity will allow you to get clear about your purpose | → | **THE RESULT** You become more intentional and feel more at peace |

How It Started with Me, Living for Others

Just trust yourself, then you will know how to live. ~Johann Wolfgang von Goethe

There have been several periods in my life when I felt lost. I spent most of my life pleasing others, so I didn't have a chance to truly discover what I wanted and what would make me happy. I didn't start making moves to fearlessly live for myself until a major shift that I had been praying for occurred at 27, and I discovered my purpose. But it wasn't easy; it was a process.

After I graduated from Howard University with a bachelor of arts in broadcast journalism along with a minor in entrepreneurship, I finally felt as if I had the time to get to know who I was at my core. It took a long time for me to realize I had bought into others' belief that what I really wanted wasn't attainable. So most of what I had accomplished and the decisions I had made reflected my acceptance that my parents' way was best. I didn't figure out what I wanted because I was so focused on satisfying them. As a child, I thought that following what my parents wanted for me would keep them happy and avoid arguments I would never win anyway. I didn't speak up out of fear of being attacked or misunderstood or simply not heard because I didn't feel like my opinion or feelings mattered much. I never felt as if I could express myself.

It also didn't help that I've always spoken with a lot of passion and emotion, which made it hard for my message to come across appropriately. And it was often misread as disrespect. My passion boiled over because of the emotions I kept bottled up inside. The moment everything began to rage inside of me, I didn't know how to respond. So I remained quiet and observant, and figured in due time that I would make them proud of me, and that would eventually be enough.

For example, I specifically pursued broadcast journalism because they agreed it was a better career goal than what I had in my heart. The first thing I wanted to pursue as a little girl was singing, but when, in my shy nature, I expressed wanting to become a singer/dancer/songwriter, I was encouraged to set aside that dream because it wasn't a secure career. I recall times when I was forced to discontinue modeling classes, gymnastics, dance team, and chorus.

After earning my degree, I was unable to find the journalism jobs I wanted, so I was encouraged to pursue a career working for the government like they did. That was when I was finally able to advocate for myself in a way I had never done before. I understood that my parents' intentions were, and had always been, coming from the right place. But I knew that was not what I was meant for. I also began to understand that my parents did what they could with what they had, but my spirit knew better. My calling was elsewhere, and I was confident that God was pushing me in the direction of what it was. So I continued to search while working whatever random odd jobs I could get, many of which were in retail or marketing.

I allowed my parents' idea of who I was and who I should be to determine how I saw myself. And to me, they had control over every aspect of my life. The way I saw it, since they provided for me, things were meant to go their way. That became normal for me. Then I realized I lived for them because I didn't trust myself. I began to understand that if I learned to trust myself, then I could learn to trust my decisions, trust that I was good enough and truly capable, trust my own strength, and then discover and reclaim my power over myself and my life. I knew that I had to let go of the need to always please others and stop suppressing and neglecting my own needs. I had to eliminate low self-esteem and believe my thoughts were important, that they mattered. More than anything, I yearned to be heard and seen, so I had to be shown that my thoughts, my feelings, my emotions were valued. That I was valued.

Living for Myself and God

Loving oneself isn't hard, when you understand who and what 'yourself' is. It has nothing to do with the shape of your face, the size of your eyes, the length of your hair or the quality of your clothes. It's so beyond all of those things and it's what gives life to everything about you. Your own self is such a treasure ~Phylicia Rashad

Once I realized I had spent the majority of my life living for others, I knew it was time to make a change. In order to feel at peace and release any unexplained anger, frustration, confusion, lack of clarity, and other heavy feelings inside, I had to uncover who I truly was. To be the most authentic version of myself and let go of emotions holding me back from that, I had to dig deep and continue on a journey to be clear with myself.

Although I underwent a specific shift when I was 27 years old, my journey to living for myself and discovering my God-given purpose began earlier than that. After graduating from Howard University,

I experienced the pressure of transitioning from a young lady to an adult. It meant that I needed a job, I needed to support myself, and I needed to reach life goals. At 22 years old, I was ashamed that I didn't have my life all mapped out and felt pressure to figure it all out at once.

Going back home after living away was a shock. It was also a shock that I didn't have a job in my field. After many internships at various television, print, and radio outlets, I thought I would have landed something by the time I graduated. But I had to work with the cards that life dealt me.

It took me about five years to go through the process that got me to where I am right now. I finally made the conscious decision to stop being a yes person and start looking out for myself. I had to get to my lowest point to start healing. To remove the guilt and shame, I had to expose my vulnerabilities and dig deep into pains of my past, confronting the people and situations that had hurt me. I was depressed for years until I couldn't suppress it any longer.

Before, I couldn't tell people that I was good or fine when they'd ask how I was doing. It took professional therapy, unearthing my past and thoughts I had about myself and others around me. I had to identify the coping mechanisms I used to deal with pain and dispose of them. After acknowledging what my challenges were, I took it a step further and made sure that I focused on my self-care routine, which included strengthening my relationship with God, being more mindful, forgiving myself, regular meditation, yoga, and praying more and more intentionally. All of these things made a difference in how I was able to receive God's messages—both directly and through my guardian angels or guides. When I started letting life happen rather than fighting it, I was able to become extremely clear about who I was and become more open for God's plan for my life and ready to receive it.

One of those moments was on Wednesday, July 30, 2014, when I was fired from the longest job I had held after graduating. I had worked as a customer service representative at a petroleum company for nearly two years, and it was a good paying position with benefits. Even though I knew it wasn't a place I was meant to be for a long period of time, getting fired initially left me devastated, humiliated, and uncertain about the future. But I could clearly see that God was pushing me out of that position because he had greater plans for me that I wouldn't be able to accomplish as a customer service representative.

I continued praying, meditating, and working on a motivational blog I had been planning to launch (www.HumbleSunshine.com). I worked hard to find a new gig in communications that would allow me to utilize my college education. Instead, in September 2014, I began teaching at the University of Mary Washington's James Farmer Scholars program and soon began to understand what God's plan had been for me all along.

I Finally Discovered My Life's Purpose

He had plans to answer my prayers to help me discover my purpose.

"For I know the plans I have for you," says the Lord. "They are plans for good and not for disaster, to give you a future and a hope. In those days when you pray, I will listen. If you look for me wholeheartedly, you will find me. I will be found by you," says the Lord. "I will end your captivity and restore your fortunes. I will gather you out of the nations where I sent you and will bring you home again to your land. (Jeremiah 29:11-14)

I have come a long way, and I succeeded against the odds by having the strength and courage to live for myself, follow my dreams, trust more, be more open to speaking my peace, and forgive myself through the process. Succeeding against the odds also meant not allowing myself to be defined by my failures and things that led me to feel ashamed and unable to advocate for myself. And it meant doing the internal work that freed me to discover my purpose.

By gaining greater clarity and comfort within myself and my relationship with God, I'm finally in a place I always anticipated. Because I let go and let God have His way in my life, I was able to discover His specific purpose for me and my life. I had always loved to help others and knew I was meant to have a big impact through my platform. However, it wasn't clear until after I began teaching that my purpose was to help women find peace and healing in their lives so they could stop making the same mistakes.

I could relate because I have had periods in my life where I felt a lack of peace and lack of clarity about who I was and what my purpose truly was. I began Humble Sunshine to mentor young girls and women and help them through providing an encouraging word, genuine guidance, or just a sympathetic ear to help them get through tough seasons or transitions in their lives. My life's purpose has become my life mission.

Where I Am Today

Learn to get in touch with the silence within yourself, and know that everything in life has purpose. There are no mistakes, no coincidences, all events are blessings given to us to learn from. ~Elisabeth Kubler-Ross

Today, I'm finally at a level of peace that I had never dreamed of. Now, I will not say that every day is perfect, but I am certainly better equipped and confident with regards to advocating for myself and being at the most peaceful place I've ever been. I'm living towards my dreams through working in my God-given purpose. I'm also effecting change and it's an amazing feeling.

Most days, I feel like I reside in a level of peace I wasn't always sure was possible for me. I can say with certainty that I have become more transparent and better able to assist others going through the same or similar things. I am able to speak more openly, not feeling like I have to always say the perfect thing and look a particular way. I have become a champion for young girls and women of all ages to help stop the cycle of low self-esteem, forced silence, and lying to ourselves and others.

I've learned that everything that has happened in my life had to happen in the way and in the time that it did to get me to this exact moment. Looking back, I see how all the good, bad, or indifferent experiences helped me learn specific lessons that aided in my growth, allowing me to become the woman I am today. Continuing to grow and learn more of life's lessons will propel me even further.

Call to Action

Infuse your life with action. Don't wait for it to happen. Make it happen. Make your own future. Make your own hope. Make your own love. And whatever your beliefs, honor your creator, not by passively waiting for grace to come down from upon high, but by doing what you can to make grace happen... yourself, right now, right down here on Earth. ~Bradley Whitford

I want you to know you should be encouraged to follow God's plan for your life. When you get still and listen, you will hear and see what God is trying to tell you, and He will lead you to understand the grand purpose of your life. Aren't you tired of feeling confused with constant mind clutter? Don't you want to feel unconditional peace?

If you are like me and have to release the chains of living your life for others, not trusting yourself or others, I encourage you to try your hardest to take the first step today. Make time today. You deserve to discover greater peace, healing, and a happier life.

If you would like to start on your journey to peace, my *Manifestation Journal (for Peace & Healing)* will get you started on your journey to your purpose. It can also be beneficial if you need to reboot your drive. With the *Manifestation Journal (for Peace & Healing)*, you'll be able to create a plan that will launch you in a positive direction. It is available at www.HumbleSunshine.com.

Other resources that could be very useful are the One-Moment Meditation, Calm, and Daily Yoga apps.

I hope that you are encouraged and inspired to pursue your passions and your dreams. Do not let the fear that you can't do it or that you'll fail or that it won't be ideal for someone else stop you.

No More Standing Still:

Taliah mustered up the courage to release her chains and found peace. The thing about peace is that once you get to that place, you never go back to how things used to be.

What do you have to let go of so that you move forward to get to that place of peace in your life? Is it feelings of inadequacies, a childhood memory, or do you need to not give up anything but step into your power and find *your* strength?

Make today the day that you no longer stand still! Taliah realized that she had to live for her, not anyone else. Who are you living for? Why are you standing in your own way? Use her story as the motivation you need to step forward into your purpose.

Chain releasing requires that you do many things: two of those require trusting yourself and trusting the process. ~Ari Squires

How will you use the mistakes you've made in your life as stepping stones?

My biggest mistake:

_____

_____

_____

_____

How I will turn that lesson into a blessing:

_____

_____

_____

About Amanda Eaddy Oliver

Amanda Eaddy Oliver is an author, educator and teen girl advocate in Prince George County, VA. Mother, Speaker and Purpose Pusher are a few more positions that she holds while living on this Earth. Each position is fueled by her desire to love people the way that Jesus Christ loves them and to help them reach their potential in Him. Amanda has been called to transform the lives of young women and children. She is passionate about encouraging, empowering, and educating these individuals in hopes that they would effectively guide their own households and create strong and unified communities.

Amanda spent the majority of her young adult life searching for love and affirmation in others. Pregnant at 19, she struggled with her identity. She understands the pressure that comes with trying to fit in, having low self-esteem, and being misunderstood. She's made poor choices, experienced physical and emotional abuse, been hurt and hurt others. Her experiences have prompted her desire to reach teen girls before they have their own families. She believes that if you strengthen and empower a girl when she is young, you provide her with the tools needed to withstand the pressures of life. Amanda uses her craft to teach lessons. Through humility and transparency, she strives to instill hope of Jesus in those who are frustrated with their current situation.

Amanda has learned that making mistakes doesn't put your life story on hold. Mistakes can be powerful when someone learns from them and makes a decision to keep going no matter what. You can begin again! The rest of her life will be dedicated to creating opportunities for this to be possible for young women and children that need it. This is her ministry! Her life's work!

Chapter 3

Becoming "Queen"

AMANDA EADDY OLIVER

-o-o-o-o-o-o-o-

A woman isn't born *knowing* that she is a queen. She doesn't automatically stare up at her mother with the realization that she too is royalty, a treasured masterpiece, irreplaceable. No matter what is poured into her soul over the years, the affirmations revealing her priceless internal beauty, she will have to travel the journey to queendom on her own. As she matures and functions in a world filled with brokenness and insecurity, she will have to force her way to the truth of how a true queen should look.

This journey isn't pretty, no matter how made-up she may be.

This journey isn't easy, no matter how strong she may seem on the surface.

This journey is painful, no matter how much she holds the medicine for others through her words, eyes, hands, and thighs. She will be broken, uncertain, and unfilled until she is forced into freedom.

This journey is mine.

Thirty-five years later, and I'm just getting it.

I choose to share now because freedom is like air; once you have it going through your soul daily, you can't live without it. I also strongly believe that transparency saves lives. The day I realized that I could breathe because I was finally free was the day I became determined to help other teen girls avoid the journey to becoming queen the way I did.

Being in bondage is unnecessary. Unfortunately, for more than 35 years, I have placed myself in chains. Numerous forms of bondage. There were so many times that I cried out to the Lord to release me, promising Him that I wouldn't return to the chains once I was free. And many times I have broken those promises.

Why? you may ask. What would make you return to something when you have been delivered?

Love.

Eaddy. Oliver. Kimbrough. The last names of three kings I have had the privilege of loving and having them love me back.

But being with a king is not enough. Not when your identity is entangled with the desire to be loved. When who loves you, how they love you, and why they love you becomes an obsession, you are in trouble. When you become depressed, suicidal and unsure why you were created because of someone's lack of love for you, you are in bondage. When your sole purpose in life is to prove to someone that you are deserving of love, you are headed towards a road of destruction.

This is a road that I know very well.

My parents named me Amanda. When I found out that it meant *deserving of love*, a shift in the wrong direction took place. I always struggled with low self-esteem. Imagine a teenage girl with a lack of confidence, falling in love with every boy that flirted with her. Becoming suicidal at a young age when she was thrown away by them. That was me.

I would take trips in my mind of us getting married, having babies, and growing old together. Now that I'm free, I realize that has been a way for Satan to keep me in bondage. Connecting with the opposite sex was never a problem for me. Even though I wasn't the popular girl, I could connect with a boy emotionally, making him feel like a king with my words and actions. Boys were automatically kings to me. They didn't have to do much to prove their worth. I treated them like royalty in hopes that they would see the queen in me and confirm my identity. I needed them to prove that I was deserving of love.

My lack of identity and desire to please a man started with the relationship with my daddy. Being an Eaddy was and is still everything to me. I always carried my daddy's last name with pride knowing that I received a lot of creativity and strength from him. Yet, his love for me was not enough. Being the oldest of five was difficult. Not being the only girl was even harder. Once my sister was born, it seemed as if I was no longer "daddy's little girl." I had to vie for his attention. I wasn't as smart as my sister. I couldn't sing like my sister. My sister's vocabulary was broader than mine. There were so many differences, and I became lost in my own insufficiencies. At 35, I have to catch myself because deep down inside, I'm still the young girl longing for my daddy's approval and praise.

It doesn't matter how old a girl gets, she will always need her father. Dads, no matter how many girls you have, they all need to believe they are the apple of your eye. They need to feel important. They need one-on-one attention. Favoritism leads to jealousy and competition among your children. That is unhealthy and damaging to the sibling relationship. You need your daughters to get along. Otherwise, when they become adult women, they end up having daddy issues.

I left my father's house fearful and unsure but determined to find my equal. I was unidentifiable in my mind. The search for my king seemed to be the only solution. I fell in love with my first husband as a high school sophomore. At 19 years old, I found myself pregnant with his son. The only option I was given was to get married. Parents—especially Christian parents—a 19-year-old doesn't know anything about marriage, especially one that doesn't know their identity and purpose. A husband can't provide that.

Forcing her into a marriage before she's ready won't make the situation better. Be proactive by being present in her life. Don't be judgmental and act as if you were not a teenager at one time. Stop being afraid to talk about sex. Explain how it doesn't equate to love. Your young queen needs to hear it from you first.

Being an Oliver was just as powerful as being an Eaddy because my first husband gave me two of the greatest gifts: my children. God has used them for the last 15 years to help me stay focused. There were times when their love worked. But there were too many times I failed them. Their father loved me and my lost soul to the best of his ability. Yet his love was not enough.

After our disconnection, I continued my journey, still uncertain of my identity and still searching for the one to open my eyes. I was in and out of relationships, sharing my body with those who didn't deserve my royalty. I will never forget connecting myself to a man old enough to be my father. It was one of the worst seasons of my life. We shared a lack of identity and purpose. I knew that the relationship was wrong but every time I tried to escape; his spirit would pull on me. I saw his potential and overlooked my busted lips, his substance abuse, the broken windows, and the disappearing acts. The days when I couldn't find him, I felt like dying. Didn't he understand that I needed him to love me?

Eventually, I was able to break free from that volatile relationship. I tried to reconnect with my first husband, but too much damage had been done. Losing him hurt me to the core, but I refused to give up. With two children, I traveled the journey on my own, focusing on their needs. Unfortunately, that didn't last long. I was an empty vessel. My voids cried out so loudly that they overrode anything else that truly mattered. More relationships filled with broken promises followed. The pursuit of happiness was nowhere in sight. No man was working. So I started drinking and smoking marijuana. These were temporary void fillers. I didn't realize there was only one solution to fulfill my need to be loved. His name is Jesus Christ.

In July 2008, I had a true encounter with Jesus Christ. An unforgettable experience. I couldn't see it back then but God was setting me up. He connected me to a ministry with a pastor who saw *me* immediately. We didn't have any history, yet he saw me. I didn't even know who I was. I remember coming to church with my friends, broken yet trying to hold it all in with a smile. I sat through the worship experience and I listened to Pastor Friend minister in a way that was different for me. His teaching of the Word made sense, and I was able to relate. That day, God proved how much He loved me by having Pastor Friend call me to the altar for prayer. I was the only one he called.

When I went to the altar, I felt like the woman at the well when she met Jesus. Pastor Friend spoke the truth about my life and my struggles at that time. Yet, he didn't know me. I knew God was real then, and He had orchestrated my connection with Pastor, First Lady, and Greater Dimensions Church for a higher purpose. It was imperative to release this chain. It was time to stop my search for love and identity. Unfortunately, I was not ready.

Parents, be patient. Just because your daughters may have an encounter with Christ and you start to see better behavior, doesn't mean that she is fully delivered. Deliverance takes time. She needs your support. That same year, I connected myself to another man who would eventually become my second husband. Becoming a Kimbrough was just as powerful as being an Eaddy or an Oliver. I had something to prove. Not so much that I was deserving of love but that I was worthy of being a wife again. Proverbs 18:22 NLT states "The man who finds a wife finds a treasure, and he receives favor from the Lord." I needed to be someone's treasure. I strived to prove that I was his good thing. He needed to see that connecting to me would bring him favor from God. And once he realized that, I would finally know my identity and feel good about myself. Ignoring the signs and the red flags that we weren't ready, I continued to push myself on him. Our relationship was fairly new. I was going to church and learning about my identity in God, how I was "fearfully and wonderfully made" (Psalms 139:14) and how much God loved me (1 John 4:10) before I truly knew Him. Slowly, I was maturing in God but that didn't erase my desire to be married. After two years of chasing him and pleading, I got my heart's desire. I became a Kimbrough. Five and a half years—that's how long my second marriage lasted before we were forced into a separation. You see, though Christ had found me, I was not ready to be anyone's wife. I was not whole and complete in Him. I wasn't equipped to handle the tests and trials that come with being a wife because I didn't have what was necessary to tackle my own demons. Never giving myself time to heal from the physical, emotional, and sexual abuse, I continued to pile other people's burdens and desires on top of my issues. I swept my daddy, lust, jealousy, and control issues under the rug and focused on everyone else's.

Though my spiritual relationship with Christ had grown, I was still that searching teenage girl. Just because you love Jesus doesn't mean that all your problems go away. There is a process to becoming whole and satisfied in Him.

Parents, please pay attention to your young queen. You may find that she is talking to one male after another. She may seem withdrawn after a break-up and then giddy again when the next one comes around. Take action. She may need to see a counselor to help her understand her worth. Don't sweep it under the rug and call it *typical teenage behavior*. Be her advocate.

In 2015, God said: *Enough!* He isolated me for nine months. And I hated it. No hanging out with my best friend. Separated from my husband. Not as close to my church family. I was depressed and suicidal. Because of my loneliness, I prematurely reconnected back to my husband hoping that I would feel better.

Externally, I looked great; internally, I was dying. That summer, I tried to commit suicide. I drove to the drug store, bought a bottle of Tylenol PM, and took it home. I had fought with my husband earlier that day. My son was upset with me as well. I couldn't keep the kings in my house happy. Because part of my identity was still tied to a king's love for me, I no longer wanted to live. In despair, I locked myself in my room with the pills and a knife. Swallowing the pills and slitting my wrists were the only answers at that point. But God and His powerful love stopped me before I could abort the mission He had for my life. He opened my eyes and performed a miracle that day, reminding me that I had a purpose in Him, not man. That He had created me to be a change agent for Him, not man. That if I trust in Him, He would show me just how necessary I am and how influential I could be even if I didn't have a man. That day I chose life and I have been choosing it ever since.

The year 2016 has been the year of rebirth for me. In 2015, when I was losing my mind, He showed me my future. He showed me how He would use my pain to help the lives of girls around the world. Everything I went through was purposeful. On July 30, 2015, I started my non-profit organization, #BrandNew, which provides resources, education, and rebuilding activities for girls ages 12–21 who have been scarred by trauma, whether it be sexual abuse, domestic violence, emotional abuse, or bullying. We also promote teen abstinence in hopes of decreasing teen pregnancy. *Books before boys* is what we live. Our girls know that they are worth waiting for. Their identity isn't tied to what they have between their legs.

You can visit www.brandneworg.com to find out how to get your young queen involved. God has called me to use my gifts to impact the world. It is imperative for you to know your daughters. Talk to them. Ask them about their day and don't accept mediocre conversations from them. Have real conversations about life. Moms, share your journey to becoming queen. Be transparent. It's okay to reveal your struggles. Be patient. Be forgiving. Don't pretend and make this journey look easy, which produces a spirit of perfectionism in them. You are their first examples. They need the truth.

Please visit http://educateme.teengirlsmatter.org/teengirlsmatt er/ to receive your FREE copy of *Inside the Mind of a Teen Girl: Five Truths Your Queen Needs You to Know*. If you are in need of further support in ensuring that your young queen reaches her intended destiny, the *Becoming Queen Academy* is a video series created and led by me through A Creative Solution, where we help young people improve their academic and emotional success through artistic expression.

> *What, after all, is the purpose of a woman's life? The purpose of a woman's life is just the same as the purpose of a man's life: that she may make the best possible contribution to the generation in which she is living, ~ Louise McKinney*

When it is all said and done, it is my hope that every queen that I meet will truly see herself and walk boldly in her assignment, unapologetically destroying the boxes that we have been placed in, and be ready and willing to teach the younger generation of queens how to get it done with or without the extra testosterone the society claims is necessary.

To the queens reading this book, just in case you have forgotten, let me remind you of who you are.

You are necessary. You hold the key to life in your womb. You are exquisite. You were created with a great purpose that no other woman on this Earth can do like you. You are desired. Not because of your physical beauty but because you possess a spiritual elegance that causes your king to thank God for your creation. You are more than enough. You don't have to pretend to be anyone else but yourself. Your intelligence is unmatched. Your wisdom is powerful. You are the epitome of God's grace, favor, and love. There is no need to settle for mediocrity.

You are royalty, majestic, and whole in the one who gave up His life so that you could change the life of your young queen. You have everything that you need to be the advocate that she needs. Use your power with boldness. Destroy the things that try to kill her identity and self-worth. Be the love and the light that will pierce through the darkness of her adolescent years. Be her sight giver, her chain breaker. I believe in your greatness.

Chains are no match for a purpose-driven, spirit-filled, and determined queen. Her confidence in her Creator destroys them before they form!

No More Letting People Define Me:

What I found interesting here is that Amanda felt that she didn't receive the love and attention she craved from her father. I'm sure he did his best, but this story can be used as a great example of the importance of a father's love, rather he is present or absent in his daughter's life.

Girls love their daddy's attention and when there is lack, naturally she seeks love and refuge in the arms of other men. They become her father, so she will do *anything* to be loved and feel appreciated. This causes her to give her body away, be abused and have children too soon.

I think this story is so powerful and I love how Amanda has used her chains to empower girls and boost their self-esteem.

To my fathers - ask yourself would you like to be the reason your daughter seeks love and attention from an abusive man who will take advantage of her? Do you realize that your love and presence in her life is vital? She looks at you as her first love. What type of example are you setting? How much love daily are you providing?

Just let that marinate, then pat yourself on the back or do better.

Fathers are daughters' only source of what love should be. If men don't set the example, she won't have one. Only a father can teach his daughter how she should be loved, respected, cared for and appreciated. Let's break this chain of father-less love. Do more. Yes, even more. Release the Chains! ~Ari Squires

How will you step in to impact a young girl's life?

_____

_____

_____

_____

When, where and how?

_____

_____

_____

_____

_____

About Cynthia Dixon

Cynthia Dixon is one of the most sought after virtual assistants. She is also as a Reiki Master Teacher and Chief Administrative Officer (CAO) whose assistance has changed the lives of many business owners.

As founder and CAO of CYNASSISTS™, a professional virtual administrative firm that provides support to C-suite executives, publicists, life coaches and entrepreneurs. Dixon is passionate about delivering premier service as she is an entrepreneur too and knows firsthand of the hard work and dedication it takes to be successful.

Dixon mentors virtual assistants, professional assistants, and entrepreneurs with the specialized knowledge she has gained throughout her 15+ year corporate career as an Executive Assistant. One of her favorite quotes is from the legendary Maya Angelou: "When you get, give; when you learn, teach." Her firm also provides social media and website management services to small to mid-sized businesses.

She takes pride in maximizing the time and work/life balance of entrepreneurs by creating successful systems that streamline their administrative needs. CYNASSISTS affords them opportunities to concentrate on their forefront and increase their bottom line. "No one should have to do it all by themselves, when they have someone qualified to assist" is the mantra.

Dixon has spent her career supporting presidents and CIOs of Fortune 500 companies. Built on the principle that entrepreneurs can ascend in their success with the right person supporting their vision, she left corporate America and created her own venture in 2014. CYNASSISTS provides entrepreneurs the critical support that provides more flexibility and family time. Dixon, too, craved to be in charge of her own destiny after the birth of her youngest son. Being in the position to give entrepreneur's access to essential tools to run their company allows reaching greater heights.

Dixon is a native New Yorker and currently resides in Maryland. She holds a Bachelor of Science from Langston University and believes in the power of service because she has seen it transform lives first hand. She knows because she cares about her legacy and how it's reflected, she can heighten the value of her client's brand that much more.

Chapter 4

Living a Life of Love

CYNTHIA DIXON

—o-o-o-o-o-o-o-o—

It wasn't until I was about seven years old when I learned my mother hated me. I know hate is a strong word, but it was her choice of words back then.

A Mother's Love

There's nothing like a mother's love. The type where she embraces and erases her child's fear with a subtle calming hand. Her presence is sacred because it's the only heartbeat they've either shared maternally or by the blessings only God can unite.

In 2016, as I prepared for my fourteen-hour return flight from Abu Dhabi on Qatar Airlines, I found I had an entire row to myself. I noticed a family in the middle aisle trying to put their exhausted child to sleep, but before our take off, he had his way. He was free to roam around within the scope of his parents, as if he had his own play area. Soon I observed the husband trying to assist his wife as she consoled their child to sleep. He made sure his wife had everything she needed. She had the baby's bottle, blanket, and her reading material, all before he buckled his seatbelt and I was reminded of my own husband and family with a grateful heart.

Shortly after the doors of the plane closed, a Muslim woman and her adorable vibrant son (who couldn't be more than a year old) occupied two of the seats in my aisle. I was no longer alone. Some would be agitated by the presence of children on a long flight but believe it or not, her son gave me life. He made me look forward to the moment I would be able to see my youngest son's eyes and smile upon my return. He had curly dark hair like my twenty-three-month-old, very inquisitive, and full of life, yet well behaved son.

Although she was exhausted, she took care of his every need before she closed her eyes or thought about getting up to use the restroom. I watched them in silence and nodded to her hoping she would know it was alright to get up, as if I was his guardian for the trip. He slept so peacefully and would smile from time to time. She was fully invested in loving her child, as a mother should be.

She and I may not have spoken the same language to exchange words, but we spoke the same "Mommy Language". She poured love into the soul of her son, as I have done with my boys – his smile convinced me of that. The light of his soul persuaded me into believing that she understood the true meaning of love and its existence. I wanted to pay her the same compliment many others have paid to me, as they have witnessed the interaction between my boys and me, and the smiles that spew from their souls. Their bond made me wish I could have sped up the time it took for me to touch down at Dulles Airport in Virginia to hug my family, but as I waited patiently for our arrival, I could only reflect on my journey as a child which made me miss my boys even more. I made a promise to myself while growing up: that my children would never know the pain of my past relationship with my mother, only a promising future. Filled with love in every waking moment, I enjoyed my amazing trip, but I missed their smiles, their confusion, and those magical and mysterious learning moments.

Most of all, I missed the empowering moments we shared as a family, where I teach them Louise Hay's mirror exercise of self-approval and self-acceptance The exercise involves picking up a small mirror, look into their own eyes to disclose how much they love the individual in the mirror, how successful their lives have been and will be. My eight-year-old does most of the mirror exercises and my almost two-year-old just kisses himself.

I share this to say that I don't know why a parent would want to miss out on that. It confuses me, and it hurts the core of my soul when a child is denied the most amazing part of living: love.

Not just any type of love – a love that includes motivation, the need to feel safe, encouragement, and guidance. A love parents should provide. Yes, unfortunately, I am all too familiar with circumstances where these positive things about motherhood were not a factor in my life. Not only were they not true, I learned as an adult that it can be a generational epidemic, if you are not aware it.

By my mother's own personal decisions, she is missing out on the growth of my boys. She is missing the little things like the monthly growth spurts and updates of my youngest son. She doesn't know he likes to read, speak Spanish, and can count to twenty in English and to ten in Spanish; that he mocks the sound of animals or that he is a genius when it comes to electronic devices. He can spell his name: J-A-X-O-N. She hasn't seen his adorable smile. He is almost two years old going on a year where we haven't spoken on the phone because her pride won't allow her to apologize to me.

She will never see past her pain and embrace love. I've learned that you meet people where they are, find their truth, and forgive them. That's where God Begins.

A Moment of Reflection

Writing this story reminds me of a night I will never forget; one specific night when I was a child. My mother had the company that consisted of my grandparents and a couple of their friends. As usual, they were drinking alcohol, smoking cigarettes, and listening to music in the kitchen area/living room. I was up to use the restroom and turned the lights off quickly so they didn't notice me. I jumped from the bathroom doorway to the other side of the hallway. It was only a couple of feet between the two. I stood in the hallway snooping like an inquisitive, curly-haired little girl does at age eight.

I remember a moment when I thought someone heard me, so I quickly covered my mouth because I started to giggle.

I was listening to music with them as if I was a part of their evening. Unfortunately, I would become a part of it. I suddenly overheard my mother telling my grandmother how she hated me. It was so random and out of the blue. I truly believed my mother had eyes in the back of her head and maybe this was the moment my snooping gig was up, but it wasn't. She had no clue of my presence in the hallway, and as I was left dumbfounded, I began to cry. Me? What did I do? As tears started to flow all of a sudden... I heard a SLAP!

It was loud and appalling. You could hear someone gasp for air, in disbelief. In that moment, time stood still. My grandmother's hand flew across my mother's face so quickly, it stopped the evening. My mother stood there stunned, and I heard my grandmother yell, "a mother should never feel that way about their own child! NEVER!" I could hear the disappointment in her voice. As she prepared to leave, my mother proclaimed that my grandmother loved me more than she loved her and that's why she hated me. She was jealous of our relationship.

I ran to my room, brokenhearted. I covered my mouth and cried into my pillow all night and into the morning so no one could hear me. I cried so much that night, my eyes started to swell, my nose clogged up and I could no longer breathe.

What do I do now? How was this possible and how was I to blame? The thought of my mother not loving me for something I didn't do crushed me. I mean, I was her second child, but I was her first daughter. Doesn't that count for something? I remember thinking if she doesn't love me, then who will? Not my father. He literally returned most of my letters, when I tried to share my unloved emotions. He never stood up to his significant other for me when they argued about how I defended my youngest sister. He just sent me to live with my grandmother.

The Pain

This just heightened the numbness. You mean to tell me I am being tormented, abused, and persecuted because of how my grandmother loved me? Isn't a grandmother's love supposed to be affectionate, generous, warm, and giving? Sure it is, just not towards me. I was the middle child and for some reason, my mother was always distant with how she showed her love for me.

I remember feeling like I was Cinderella before she became a princess. She made me do everything by myself. I cooked and had to clean the entire house, even if she was home all day. I did my homework, and then looked after my sister to help her.

It all made sense now, as I look back. Her hate for me was clearly bigger than she would ever admit to. Her pain forbids her to love me the way I needed. She has too much pride to show any signs of weakness or admit to any wrongdoing. According to my mother, she was always right and everything needed to be done her way or she would lash out at you.

This hate was about her and her journey with her mother, but it also had many components to it. I don't know if I represent what she cannot admit and take responsibility for, or if she is reliving the trauma by putting me in her position as daughter.

How This Pain Has Shaped Me

The story of my recent life makes more sense than the overall story of my life. As a child, I thought I could show her I was worthy of her love so I "danced". I wasn't a ballerina or anything but I put on the best "tap dancing" shoes you could have ever imagined. In everything I did, I tried to gain her approval. My dancing consisted of showing her I was worthy of her love by cleaning the house to her expectations, graduating high school early, studying abroad, making the dean's list and by being the first to graduate college in my entire family. I even helped raise my sister... the list goes on and on.

Cleaning was her element, so I made it mine. I made it a point to give her something to brag about, but it was not enough. Her friends gave me more praise than she would ever express in my lifetime.

I remember a time back in college where I called and asked her for gas money. I never called on her because she was the type of person who threw anything she did in your face. But I needed it, so I asked. Figured if I asked for $20 until I got paid, it would not be a big deal. I held three jobs, but she just flat out told me no. She actually thought I was up to something. She was convinced that I was lying about needing money and I was trying to pull a fast one on her.

In 1998, on Mother's Day, my grandmother died and all my mother could tell me was about how I was my grandmother's favorite. That was her way of consoling me. She tried to make me feel guilty of it, but I was grateful.

She was so traumatized that she couldn't seem to stop reliving her own experience as a daughter by projecting her hurt onto me. Nothing was ever enough for her.

As an adult, I later learned why. According to my aunt, my mother was an amazing daughter. I learned that she too owned a pair of "tap dancing" shoes. As I have been told, my mother did everything to gain the approval of my grandmother, as I did with her. She was forced to grow up, leaving the little girl inside behind, without a voice because she could not articulate her expectations or take a stance as a child. Without forgiveness, she will always be that little girl inside who was left to fend for herself screaming, "WHAT ABOUT ME?" in her adult life. Her ultimate problem is an inability to look at herself and forgive, so she lashes out at me, withholding love because she did not get any herself.

I get it. Over the years, I have been able to tip-toe my way around her childhood and although she does not speak about it, she did reveal to me that she was embarrassed of her past.

Through counseling, journaling, and a plethora of self-help books like the *"Four Agreements"* by Don Miguel Ruiz, Louise Hay's *"You Can Heal Your Life"*, *"Codependent No More"* by Melody Beattie, I've learned the difference between the reality of love and how I experienced it. I learned I am the only person I can control. Everything about how others treated me wasn't about me, it was about them.

I learned to release it. I empathized with her journey as a child, from a mother's perspective. Her hate for me had nothing to do with me, it was about her. It's not like she didn't love me, she loved me in her own way. It was also the first time I met her. I met her where she was; through the soul of her pain and despite my relationship with my mother, I still love and pray for her always, just at a distance. I may not agree with her ego or her disinterest in our relationship. She still can't love me, and although I danced for her, took her on trips around the world or bought her nice things, I broke the generational pain by forgiving her. I forgave her, forgave myself, and now I am free. I released the shame, the lack of love, and don't make excuses for her absence in my journey.

"Without no struggle, there can be no progress." Frederick Douglass's powerful words have been embedded in my memory, in every moment of hardship. According to many, I wasn't supposed to succeed. Instead of wallowing in the delays, problems, or hurdles in my life, I always knew things were going to get better because God was always present in my pivots of change. The vision I had for my life could not have come true easily and effortlessly, or without obstacles and struggles. The bigger the vision I had for myself, the tougher the challenge. What I learned through the Laws of Attraction was the longer I lingered in it or put energy towards it, the longer it remained in my life. So when you are face to face with an obstacle, accept its presence, say thank you and then release it. It's the only way to move on to the next lesson. Be persistent to succeed, giving up should never be an option.

Full Circle

My trip from Abu Dhabi was an exit from my past. My moments on the plane, reliving my relationship with my mother helped me wave goodbye and I ran to my present and future: my precious boys as they waited for me in the baggage claim. Because I chose to live a life of love, to parent, to realize my purpose, and in some lucky cases, to do something after that realization, I embarked on a journey as an entrepreneur and gave life to CYNASSISTS.

The courage and persistence to keep going on, passing hurdles and obstacles, is powered by purpose. Your purpose. My purpose happened to be assisting people so that they can ascend in life, personally and in business. In all that I do or all that I've done, I have been fascinated and engulfed in roles that supported people in their journey or professionally where I supported Top Tier Executives, VPs, and CIOs.

When you have a passion for assisting others, you don't want to stop. Even when I was laid off due to an office move in corporate America, I wasn't done with supporting the vision of others. The desire to take them to the next level in their life was not fulfilled and so much bigger than me. I want to heal the world with my light or let you know you don't ever have to journey alone.

I know my past plays a part in why I started CYNASSISTS. It is a virtual assistant company that maximizes the time and balances work/life of entrepreneurs by providing administrative support, social media, and website management. It also provides a "Pick my Brain" session for virtual assistant or entrepreneurs new to owning a business. CYNASSISTS plays a part because I find myself giving all that I wasn't given as a child to others in need. It gives me an opportunity to teach, mentor, encourage and motivate, support a vision, and provide a listening ear, loyalty and love. Maya Angelou teaches us that "When you learn, teach; when you get, give."

When you find work that matters, work that you love, you won't have to work another day of your life. You'll just be having fun all the time! Assisting others is my life's purpose; it's what I've been called to do. I just do it virtually with CYNASSISTS. I get the best of both worlds.

Do what you're good at, but you never have to do it alone. Delegate or automate (or maybe even ignore) the other things that you can afford to, and you won't ever run the risk of giving up with

CYNASSISTS by your side. Let me pour into you, as you have in the service of others.

Push past whatever is keeping you from being the best version of yourself and live in your purpose. The world is waiting, as it was waiting for me. Follow my link bit.ly/Pivotal_Pieces to receive your FREE Guide: 7 Pivotal Distractions Every Entrepreneur Should Identify and walk into the journey of success you were destined to receive, so that you can service the lives of others. You can't assist anyone if you are still broken. Choose to invest in yourself today by scheduling your free 30-minute consultation at www.cynassists.com and let's see if we are aligned to ascend in our success together!

I now boldly live a life of love and my life's purpose is passing that love to my clients so they can focus on doing what they love.

No More Blame:

Cynthia takes us through an incredible story of how her life story pivoted her into her life purpose. This is a great evaluation for us all to do, because our past stories, pains and struggles that we thought would kill us, have made us be who we are today. What matters is how you transform the pain. Do you allow the pain to break you down or build you up?

Bringing purpose to your life is a practice of living from your heart and being your truth.

Purpose is not a 'doing' thing, although many of us think of it that way. We think about what we need to do to find purpose. We think of it as a career or a calling that we must follow.

Yes, your purpose can and most likely will flow into your career, but your purpose is really about who you are being. Yes, it can encompass doing, but it starts with being. It starts with discovering who you are.

> *Your purpose is whatever you love to do. Whatever brings you joy. Whatever you feel pulled and moved to do with your life. It does not have to be one set thing, and it can take many shapes or forms. But simply living your purpose is living what you love. ~Ari Squires*

Below is a purpose exercise that will help you dig deep into your life story and find a purposeful career that you were meant for. Being words: The 2 ways of being or qualities I most want to embody are:

_____

_____

_____

_____

_____

Feeling words: The 2 feelings I want to experience the most are:

_____

_____

_____

_____

_____

Doing words: The 2 things that make me feel that way the most are:

_____

_____

_____

_____

_____

You are now going to use these words to write your purpose statement by adding them in to the sentence below.

MY PURPOSE IS TO EXPERIENCE (feeling word 1) & (feeling word 2) BY BEING (being word 1) & (being word 2) AND THROUGH (doing word1) & (doing word 2).

Here is an example:
My being words are: 1) authentic and 2) inspiring
My feelings words are: 1) freedom and 2) joy
My doing words are:
1. sharing truthful message with the world through speaking & training and
2. empowering women to be their best through coaching.

So, my purpose statement would be
MY PURPOSE IS TO EXPERIENCE freedom & joy BY BEING authentic & inspiring AND THROUGH sharing truthful message with the world by speaking & training AND empowering women to be their best through coaching.

MY PURPOSE STATEMENT

Fill in the blanks to complete your purpose statement. If when you read it, it does not feel right, tweak some of the words of it until you feel happy with it.

MY PURPOSE IS TO EXPERIENCE _____

& _____ BY BEING _____

& _____ AND THROUGH _____

_____

_____ AND _____

_____.

About Theresa Alexis

Theresa Alexis is the owner and CEO of Alexis & Crew Wedding Planning and Photography and educator, author, and speaker at Theresa Alexis. Theresa Alexis was born and raised in Birmingham, Alabama where she resided until she was 18 years old. After turning 18, she joined the military. During her military career, Theresa reached and surpassed many goals she set for herself to include graduating with a certification in Professional Bridal Consulting. She also met and married her husband while serving with him in North Carolina. Her passion for weddings started shortly after her own wedding and only grew stronger over the years.

Once she moved overseas, she began to venture into photography and design and merge it with her love of weddings, love and romance. This is how the vision started and Theresa soon realized that this was her purpose. She didn't know how or when she was going to do it, she just knew she had to. Theresa began planning for life after the military and from there it all just happened so fast. Soon Alexis & Crew was established and has been building ever since. It was the push she needed to expand into writing, educating, and speaking. Theresa currently resides in Southern Mississippi with her husband and three children.

Chapter 5

From the Ashes: Rising Above Obstacles

THERESA ALEXIS

-⦿⦾⦿⦾⦿⦾⦿⦾-

"When you grow up and come back here, if you say something I don't like, I'll shoot you in the head and spit on you as I watch you fall!" Words I heard often from my father as a child. Out of all my siblings, I was the only one beaten on, kicked, slapped, spit on, and called horrible names. I grew up in a small town called Ensley inside of Birmingham, Alabama. There were eight of us total, but only seven of us lived together in the small two bedroom, 1 bath house my parents owned. I never considered that place home, as it never felt that way and I never intended to stay there past the age of eighteen. Out of five children, I was the middle child, often referred to as the knee baby.

My parents were married, but the only emotions they ever showed toward each other were anger and hate. There was no love, encouragement, or peace where I grew up. Forgiveness was like profanity in our home. My parents held a grudge towards everyone and burned almost all family bridges. My mom was more verbally abusive than my father was, but was still somewhat physically abusive. My father, on the other hand, was the main source of all the abuse I faced which includes physical, emotional, verbal, and mental. He often referred to me as a B**** and said I would never be anything in life. He even smashed my head through the glass in the front door and I was blamed for his actions.

My parents told stories of how bad I was, but never said what they had done to me to cause me to act this way. They seriously acted as if they were these perfect, model parents. Maybe in a twisted way, they somehow thought they were showing me love. I just wanted real love and affection like any other child craves. Since I couldn't get the positive attention I craved and desired, I acted out negatively and became a victim of my situation. I often felt rejected and abandoned by my parents throughout my childhood because of their fakeness, deep anger, and the hurt they may have had from their own childhood. They completely destroyed what would have been strong sibling relationships out of their anger and hurt. It was a hard life growing up as my siblings and I paid for our parent's bad choices, anger, and the ancestral curses to which they fell victim.

My siblings have a few emotional scars from seeing me beaten and thrown on the floor as if I was a criminal from the street. My older sister was the only one really old enough to remember most of what happened to me. The only thing I'm thankful about in regards to my childhood is that no one else had to endure what I did. None of my siblings had to be beaten down like I was or be called horrible names like me. While I cannot account for what happened once I left, I can surely say that no one endured the physical and mental anguish I went through when I was there. I just hope that one day my parents will truly repent for what they did and do better for themselves. It's never too late.

I never experienced love or security in my home, so when I reached my teenage years I turned to the streets, clubs, or whatever/ whoever would give me attention. I stole from a loved one because we were so poor and couldn't even afford the bare necessities. That was hurtful to her and to me, but it didn't necessarily stop me from doing it.

My parents were deacons and they took us to church, but when we came home, it was as if we never went. They'd be cursing, yelling, calling us stupid N****** and all kinds of bad words. I didn't believe in God, and wanted so badly to get out of my parent's house, my situation, and the neighborhood in which I lived. I would do anything to get away from them and make a better life and situation for myself. This is what gave me the drive to do better and be better.

I turned my attention to my schoolwork and made sure I got good grades so that I could get a scholarship to college. I sold sandwiches at school for one dollar to be able to afford uniforms for myself and get through the school year. I guess you can say that I was an entrepreneur all along without realizing it.

I joined the military, the United States Marine Corps to be exact, to get away from my parents and their toxic actions. I choose this branch because I wanted a complete life changing event to happen within me and I wanted a hardcore challenge. Going through those weeks of boot camp changed me both physically and mentally. It made me stronger and more self-disciplined. It gave me the courage to endure hardships and the bravery to stand for what I believe in, no matter the cost. I also got a sense of pride for defending my country. New friendships and mentorships were developed and I had a new family and place to call home.

I achieved and surpassed the military goals I set for myself, which have set the path for me today. While I was serving in the military, something amazing happened, God found me.

That experience changed my life and gave me the ability to forgive those who hurt me and ask for forgiveness from those I hurt. It wasn't easy to do, but I knew it had to be done in order for me to move forward in my life and new relationships.

I met and married an amazing, supportive man who I love with all my heart. He is also a Marine who served two combat tours. I'm proud of him and so thankful for such a stand-up man like him. We are still together today celebrating nine years together and eight years married. We have 3 adorable children and 2 angel babies in heaven. All 6 of these people have been a blessing to my life and have helped me be a better woman.

Honestly, I used to grieve my past and the love I felt I missed out on while growing up. I would complain about it, vent about it, and be angry about it, but why? Why should I hold on to grudges and become bitter like my parents are? Why should I be a victim when I have the power to be so much more than that? Why should I give someone else control and power over my life and cause me to become what they have called me or said I should be? They don't deserve that power. They can't hinder me from greatness unless I allow them to. It's up to me and to you to build upon our house (ourselves) and to be what we are called to be. We have a greater purpose than we think we do. We weren't created just to live, breathe, and survive. We have vision, mental strength, driven purpose, and are called to go beyond the limits we put on ourselves.

Instead, I began to use my past to give me the drive to pursue my dreams every single day, even when I may not necessarily feel like it. No one in my family had really "made it" or did anything positively impactful, so I decided to be the change I wanted to see. This is one of the many reasons I joined the military. It gave me a stepping-stone that set the course for my life being something more of purpose and vision. I didn't grow up with parents who modeled a godly or strong marriage for me to emulate, so I decided to change that and be the best example my kids needed to see. I fall short constantly in my marriage and as a parent, but I'm not afraid to admit it to them and ask for forgiveness when I've made a mistake. It is important that during life we don't hold onto hurt, pain, etc. We must quickly forgive and ask for forgiveness so that we can move towards higher and better things. We have to learn how to use those things meant for bad for good to help others release their chains, shackles, etc.

Learning this has given me the courage to establish my own business in wedding planning and wedding photography Alexis & Crew. I want to impart something great into couples who are starting their journey as husband and wife and give them a beautiful day to establish lifelong happiness as newlyweds and beyond. I want to pour into them so that they can do the same for others.

I'm very passionate about the marriage covenant and what it truly means to be in a marriage, start a family, and building your own family legacies and traditions. Marriage is so important and sacred to me, which is the number one reason I became a wedding planner. I believe that all marriages can make it long term and can be fulfilling. I use my business as a platform to encourage brides and grooms about the process of marriage and how it's a continual process, not a one-time event (e. g. the wedding day).

This eventually branched off and gave me a voice to speak out and encourage others and I'm currently building my brand as Theresa Alexis, educator, author, and speaker. I am an educator to those who are struggling to find their voice in this rather noisy world. Whether it's in the wedding industry or in general; an author and speaker of inspiration, knowledge, and rising to your inner power. This is my platform for encouraging everyone: business owners, clients, etc.

I love the quote, "If you can believe it, then you have the ability to achieve it" (my paraphrasing). You have to refuse to stay stuck in your situation and choose to live life fully and make a difference to yourself and others.

The change starts with you and then you can plant these same seeds into your kids, husband/wife, business, friends, etc. Use your God-given voice to get people to hear you in a unique way. There is no other way around it, it has to come from within you and be genuine and authentic. You can't allow things or people to stop you.

"Be a true hustler" has been such a blessing to hear throughout my adult life. Keep the heart and don't lose focus of the goal ahead.

The most powerful thing I've ever read was a post by my business coach, Ari Squires, that said, *"Anyone can take the hand you were dealt and win with it"*. Now THAT is truth and has helped me to pick myself up so many times when I felt like quitting and giving up.

The moral of my story is this: you do not have to fall victim to any situation or circumstance. You have the power for change embedded within you; it's just waiting to be awakened. You can overcome any obstacle and be who you desire to be. The journey will be hard, the journey will be long, but it will be so worth it in the end. Anyone can motivate you, tell you a good story, and give you awesome quotes, but if you don't desire to change yourself first then you don't want it bad enough. YOU have to want it bad enough. It has to be a daily decision on your part to make your dreams happen. Don't wait on family and friends to help you. Don't expect people to pave the way for you. Be the one who helps yourself and pave the way for others. Nothing is subject to change if we just sit around and wait for others. Do more and be the change by stepping out of your comfort zone and investing in yourself (education, mentorship, etc.). You won't lose unless you decide to give up.

My prayer and hope is that we will all rise up to our true calling and go beyond our potential. That we will desire change, be a change, and encourage others to make a change. Break free from the things that are constantly holding us back and run full speed ahead to pursue our destiny. Change is inevitable when we release the chains of any obstacles holding us back.

This is why I am so passionate about helping military brides have the most memorable experience possible. After all, I've been through, it has led me to this and I want to share something very special with you.

If you are getting married soon, download my free gift. It will help you determine how to select the best vendors. It's available at: https://vr2.verticalresponse.com/s/3quicktips

No More Staying Down:

Theresa said something very powerful. She said she had to forgive. This was what gave her strength to move past her hurt and pain. I believe that forgiveness is the ultimate act of love. It's love for the people who hurt us and for ourselves.

Once you sit in that power of forgiveness, Theresa says you can then walk according to God's will for your life. This is true when you walk and serve in purpose, and there is no greater feeling than having this type of freedom. Forgiveness releases you from bondage.

We all have something we haven't let go of. On a subconscious level, the energy of holding on to pain only holds you back because it doesn't serve you or nurture you. I invite you to finally release the density of the pain that is keeping you in chains from moving into your passion, purpose, and joy and experience the expansive freedom that true forgiveness can offer.

It's never too late to forgive. If you hold on to the pain, you allow your circumstance to define you.

It is easy to lose ourselves in the emotions of our relationships, but the more we can take a broader and spirit-focused view, the more easily we can ride through our challenges with grace and an open heart.

These principles may help:
- The other person is your teacher. They are helping you better understand yourself. When they trigger you, ask yourself "What is this showing me about myself?" or "How can I grow through this situation?" or "What is the lesson in this for me?"
- Clear the emotion and then respond. Be aware of communicating when you are high on emotion and coming from a reactive space. Rather than projecting your reaction onto that person, take some time out to own it, feel it and process it before you respond. Speak from your calm, neutral center.
- Be willing to witness your ego. Watch how you move into a space of fear, need, control, anxiety, manipulation, guilt tripping, anger etc. Witness these patterns, but don't judge yourself.

- Keep your heart open and filled with love. Rather than holding heavy feelings like anger, blame, and resentment in your heart; instead, practice forgiveness, send that person some love, and it let go.
- Honor and love yourself. Know what you deserve. Ask for what you truly want. Respect yourself, your body, and your time. Find the courage to speak what you feel, even when you feel vulnerable.
- Let go when it's time to let go. If it is time for someone to leave your life, be strong and brave and let them go. You are simply just making space for something even better to come along.

Fill up your inner cup and overflow with self-love. Turn to your self-care practices if you need support. Journal, get into nature, call up your friends, have a bath, watch a funny movie and love yourself. Make sure your inner cup is full.
~Ari Squires

What family member do you need to forgive?

_____

_____

_____

_____

_____

Write your commitment today to move past the pain.

_____

_____

_____

_____

_____

Transforming Mental Chains

Artwork by Seo Yong-Deon

www.liquidartsysem.com

I had reasoned this out in my mind, there was one of two things I had a right to, liberty or death; if I could not have one, I would have the other.
~Harriet Tubman

About Erica Hill

Erica Hill is a certified financial educator instructor and certified life coach affectionately known as the "Generational Money & Wealth Mentor™". She provides both mentoring and coaching services to her clients. Throughout the course of her career, she has helped female entrepreneurs dig themselves out of financial ditches, upgrade their money mindsets, and create financial plans for their business and family.

As the author of Money Management Strategies for Kids, and the founder of the non-profit organization Caring Loyal Advocates Supporting Society (CLASS), she has become known as a trusted partner for anyone seeking greater levels of financial, spiritual, and personal satisfaction. Erica is a well-known expert in the field of finance, and she has helped thousands of women and their families begin to build generational wealth.

Erica holds a bachelor's degree in Business Finance from Clark Atlanta University. When she's not in the office or with clients, she enjoys traveling, spending time with friends and family, attending jazz concerts, meditating, and taking a walk through the local park.

Chapter 6

It's Time to Ditch Those Fears Surrounding Money

ERICA HILL

---◦◦◦◦◦◦◦◦---

"You know life for me ain't been no crystal stair. It's had tacks in it, and splinters, and boards torn up, and places with no carpet on the floor bare" –Langston Hughes

This is one of my favorite quotes. It is a statement that I can so much relate to because it summarized my story coming up as a child, and my mindset around money. As an advocate for generational wealth, I thought it fit to share how our mindset surrounding money keeps us in bondage; and it usually stems from our childhood experiences. As I share my story with you, I want you to think about your own money story. I think you will see some resemblance and then we can release the chains as a generation.

I grew up in a low to middle-class family. My parents divorced when I was ten and I went to live with my grandmother, but my parents remained a part of my life. I would only see my father in the summers because he lived in a different state. I would see my mom on a regular basis because she lived in the same city my grandmother lived in.

My mom had 4 children by the age of twenty-two and when my parents decided to get a divorce; my grandmother relieved my mom of some of her financial stress from being a single parent by raising the oldest kids which were my sister and me. If you were on the outside looking in, you would think that my sister and I had the best of everything because my grandmother made sure that we were well dressed, well fed, and well educated, but this was the furthest thing from the truth. We were lacking an essential thing which was financial education.

Yes, we were educated according to the school system. We both graduated from high school and I went on to get a degree from Clark Atlanta University. But the education we lacked was being good stewards over our money. For some reason, everyone forgot this part.

No one sat down to teach me anything about money. My grandmother didn't teach me, my parents didn't teach me, the schools didn't teach me, the university that I graduated from didn't teach me. This was by far the most important thing that I think I could have learned because if someone would have started to teach me the importance of money around the age of five, I guarantee you I would be a millionaire by now. However, I was taught to go to college and get a degree to make more money.

The funny part was that no one taught me what to do with the money once I made it. So, I listened. I was very obedient. I graduated from college with a degree in Business, but as I walked across the stage to get my degree, bad credit walked with me.

My sophomore year in college, they offered the college students credit cards. So as soon as I received my card I went to the mall. Man, I maxed that card out. Did I forget to mention that I didn't have a job? So guess what happened... Bad credit here I come.

At the age of twenty, I ended up with so much bad credit and was in credit card debt. Stay with me now because the story gets better. My degree was in Business Finance and in the financial industry, the first thing they do when you're applying for a job is pull your credit. It took me 4 years to go to college to get a degree and seven years to clear up my credit problems.

Now I have this job but I still have not learned how to be a good steward over money and this is the first real job I have ever had. When I would get paid, I would go shopping. I didn't cook, so I ate out a lot. I loved to be entertained so I was forever going to various social events. I can truly say that I would ball out of control until it was time to pay my bills and I didn't have enough money. Then the emotions of fun quickly turned into panic, fear, anxiety, stress, and depression (just to name a few). I started to feel like a failure.

When I looked at my bank account and it said insufficient funds, I knew that I was not going to receive another check for a week, so then I had to borrow from 'Paul to pay Peter.' I would pay some bills now, and then I had to wait until the next paycheck came so I could pay other bills. It's like I always ended up in the RED: I couldn't escape the debt.

This continued to happen for at least three or four years. For some reason, I could not figure out how to get off this financial roller coaster. I saw my friends around me with the designer handbags and clothes; so I wanted them too. I didn't want to feel less by not having the materialistic things that they had. Let's face it. We all had degrees; therefore, I wanted to remain equal.

When they went on vacations, I wanted to go too. I found myself always wanting to be "a part of the crowd". It seemed to me that material things brought them happiness and that was something that I wanted as well.

They could go to a club and "make it rain" throwing money away in a carefree manner. My identity became wrapped around material things and less around anything with substance.

To make matters worse, my boyfriend came from a privileged upbringing, so he was used to buying expensive things as well. He was always showering me with gifts and I wanted to do the same things for him. But he wouldn't accept inexpensive items as a gift. If it didn't cost a certain amount; he really didn't want it. So hey... I had a facade to keep up.

I started noticing that the things that I thought were supposed to bring me happiness started to do anything but... I was always depressed, stressed, worried and fearful. I got to the point where the only things I wanted to do were eat and go to sleep because debt had taken over my life.

I started to put on a lot of weight in the process and then I started to withdraw from people. The fun times that I used to have started to become few and far between. The feelings grew worse every time I looked at my bank account and had no money saved. I really started to feel like a complete loser.

I would go to work and my co-workers would be talking about the things that they did over the weekend and all of my stories would be like, "yeah I didn't do anything, I just slept."

Then one day, it hit me... I had fallen into a deep state of depression and it all stemmed from my financial situation, or so I thought. Somewhere and somehow, I had lost myself. I was no longer this fun, "happy go" lucky person that I was before. I had turned into this secluded bitter woman that only sat around and complained. I could not allow this to continue so I really started to seek counsel through prayer.

One thing that I was taught is when everything else fails, take it to God and this is what I did. I started to go to church more and I really got connected to the word (my bible). As my faith grew stronger, I noticed that my situation started to change and my outlook on life started to shift. I no longer saw myself as a victim but as the conqueror. I also started to change my circle of friends, including the guy that I was dating.

I started to want more for myself. So I quit my job and found a better one in the mortgage industry. I started to see people my age buying houses. Never before was homeownership even something I thought about, but when I was put into an environment where this was common, it became common to me as well. I felt like if Sallie can buy a home, so can I.

So I started to do everything that I needed to do to purchase a home. The first thing I did was work on my mindset. I also started to put systems in place that would allow me to become a homeowner and this included working on getting my credit better and saving for a down payment.

I created a budget and I would not go outside of it no matter what. The old habits of balling out of control no longer existed *but* one thing that I would still do was treat myself to something nice at least once a month. I didn't want to ever feel as if I was totally depriving myself; however, I made sure that I did not accumulate any more debt. I knew that my debt to income ratio had to stay within reason in order for me to get approved for my house. The days of living paycheck to paycheck had ended.

I also became aware that the problem wasn't the amount of money that I was making. I always felt like if I made more money, I would not be so stressed, but that was not the issue. The issue was the amount of money that I was spending. I would see people that made less money than I made in my early twenties buying a house. It was because they were being good stewards of their money. They were not carrying the debt load that I was carrying then.

It became very clear to me that my self-worth was not in material things. Out of all the material things that I felt was important at that time, I could not use any of these items towards the purchase of my home. I mean, these were not appreciating assets. They were not assets at all. Frankly, they became liabilities.

Change Yourself for Change

At that point, I began to study the patterns of wealthy people. People like Warren Buffet, Bill Gates, and Michael Bloomberg. I started to understand that the real secret to wealth is having multiple streams of income.

I started to change my circle of friends. I no longer surrounded myself with people that talked about how much money they were going to spend and replaced them with people that talked about how much money they were going to invest. I started to see the glass as half full instead of half empty. I started to disassociate myself with my childhood *money story* which was *money doesn't grow on trees, and we can't afford this or we can't afford that, or you have to work really hard in order to make money.* I really got present to the fact that this type of mindset breeds lack and scarcity. If you hear it enough, it becomes stored into your subconscious mind and if you are not really careful, you will start to believe it and act it out into your life.

This was the story that I gravitated to in my early twenties because I didn't understand the power of thoughts. I also didn't understand the power of shifting your paradigm. I didn't see anyone in my family that was extremely wealthy, so I never thought that this could be a possibility for me. But once I released the CHAINS of my poverty mindset; I started to build generational wealth.

I purchased my first home at the age of twenty-seven. I then went on to become a Real Estate Investor. Now I am the author of Money Management Strategies for Kids (Secrets Parents Must Know about Kids and Money). I am a certified financial education instructor, speaker, coach, and founder of a Non-Profit organization for youth development. I coach parents, specifically mothers, on how to teach their kids about money. I also teach moms how to ditch their fears surrounding money so that they can start living life without limitations.

How My Story Can Change Generations

I realize my story was meant to be told to inspire others and show them that there can be light at the end of the tunnel. It doesn't matter where you are in life, nothing is permanent. To be born poor is not by choice, but to die poor is. You can change any situation no matter how gloomy it may seem. All it takes is a plan and action.

Once you become authentic to who you are and fall into alignment with this, everything else will fall into place.

Chains can only prevail if you allow them. The only chain there is, is the chain in your head. Once you become aware of this, you can move on from your past and embrace your future. Remember to take pleasure in the present. That's what you will have to do and often times that's not easy for most of us.

Even though you may not be where you want to be for now, start to become thankful for your journey. Take pleasure in focusing on the things that you do have and give 'Thanks'. Once you start coming from a place of gratitude, your journey will become lighter and brighter.

If you need help teaching your kids how to be good stewards of money but you feel as if you are not financially confident yourself, please visit my website at bit.ly/moneytips4kids. I have included a free download of tips that you can teach your kids about money at any age. These tips will help navigate your kids on their way to becoming financially responsible adults.

If you need help managing your own money, please visit bit.ly/mybudgetsheet. Here you will find a free budget sheet that will help you to become a good money manager over your finances.

My biggest dream for humanity is that generational wealth can be more than just a thought; it can be your REALITY regardless of how you started out in life. NOW LET'S RELEASE THOSE CHAINS, WE'VE HELD ON TO THEM LONG ENOUGH!

No More Fears Surrounding Money:

I am so grateful for Erica's transparency. It takes a big person to say they were not responsible with their money. I would love you to sit for a few seconds with your money story and reflect on how it has caused you to make certain decisions in your life.

What did you learn about money as a child?

_____

_____

_____

_____

_____

Do you pass those same money fears to your children or family? How?

_____

_____

_____

_____

_____

What can you do differently so that you don't pass this cycle down to future generations?

_____

_____

_____

_____

_____

About Patricia Clement

Patricia Clement is the founder and owner of JumpStarz Jump Rope Lessons. JumpStarz is a jump rope company that services Central Virginia and the surrounding areas. JumpStarz teaches children and adults how to jump single, long, and double-dutch jump rope.

Patricia is a devoted wife, mother of two, has 19 years of law enforcement experience, sworn Police Officer and successful entrepreneur. Patricia mentors for the Richmond Big Brother, Big Sister program, an Amateur Athletic Union (AAU) Coach and avid *couponer*. Patricia is a recipient of the 2015 Allen, Allen & Allen Hometown Hero award and has received numerous awards for serving her community. Patricia has a passion for helping people and is an excellent role model for young girls.

In 2012 Patricia launched Jumpstarz, LLC and has since shared her gift with hundreds of children and adults. As a result of her efforts, she is also credited with creating employment opportunities for her 12 employees.

Chapter 7

Flipped My Flaws

PATRICIA CLEMENT

-o-o-o-o-o-o-o-o-

Flaw: (of an imperfection) mar, weaken, or invalidate (something).

Flip: to turn (something) over

I'm not really into astrology, but I must admit I am truly *fire* as my Sagittarius sign describes me—feisty and exciting.

Sagittarian women are referred to being the wild child of the zodiac. Adventurous, fun loving, sociable, and friendly, they are typically determined to live life to the fullest. Inspiring and spontaneous, this is an honest woman, a straight shooter who speaks her mind. Those who prefer a subtler approach to life can sometimes consider them too aggressive or impatient because she values independence and freedom, manifested both in a liberal open-mindedness and a dislike of feeling trapped or obligated.

I was born on December 1, 1972, in Brooklyn, New York. I'm the youngest of five, with two older brothers and two older sisters. I have a different father than my four siblings, who are all two years apart in age, but there's a six-year gap between me and the youngest. So they basically grew up together in the same house with my mom and their dad until he passed away. Their father was described as an alcoholic who physically abused them when he wasn't beating on my mom. Six years after becoming a widow, while working at a hospital as a nurse's aide, my mom met a man named Tangeray and got pregnant with me.

I spoke to him a few times, but I began to dislike him because he never kept his promises. I met him in person at the age of 16 and found out he was married with other kids, and I was supposed to be a secret. After learning that, it all made sense. Now I understood why my older brothers used to call me an accident instead of Pat. Of course, being the youngest of five, I was often beaten, tortured, and slung around by my brothers. Especially the youngest one who's six years older than me. Man, he used to give me skin burns, (when someone grabs your wrist with both hands and twists your skin in opposite directions). He used to practice wrestling moves on me and just straight up treated me like the mistake/accident they said I was. Now that I think about it, I guess my mom told my siblings that I was an accident or mistake. And although most siblings pick on younger siblings, those childhood memories are the reason I'm not close to my brother today as an adult.

Since my siblings were all older than I was, I grew up closer to friends my age. In 1980 after a house fire, we moved to 514 Warwick Street, also in Brooklyn. I remember being excited as we walked through the new, bigger apartment but then being disappointed when I counted three bedrooms. I knew my two sisters would share a bedroom, my two brothers would share a bedroom, and the last bedroom was for my mom and me, since I was the youngest.

But Warwick Street was where I met two of my best friends: Tammy Cole aka Tam and Sandra Boulder. I love these girls dearly, and I'm proud to say we're still good friends and refer to each other as sisters. What a blessing to be friends for 36 years with no fights, no *I ain't speaking to her*, and we never slept with one another's man.

Tam, Sandra, and I were inseparable. I didn't have a big family, so I always hung with them. We would play together all day then beg our moms to let us stay the night at each other's house. Sandra's home was the best. I didn't have my own bed, and Tam never had hers, so we always wanted to stay at Sandra's. We grew up jumping double-dutch all day; getting wet in the Johnny pump (fire hydrant); and playing tag, skelly, kick the can, and red light/green light 123.

When I was 11, Tam and I were getting ready to board the charter bus for her family reunion somewhere down south.

Tam said, "Let's drink a beer."

We always saw adults drinking during bus trips, and we thought this was something that's supposed to be done. *Man*, we went to the corner store, bought a quart of Old English (Old E), and two plastic cups. We loved the silly feeling beer gave us. We sat in the back of the bus and giggled until we fell asleep. Our next 15 years would be forever changed.

Growing up in Brooklyn was very fast-paced. By the time I started seventh grade, I was both drinking and carrying a gun. Once we started drinking, we began to hang out. Once we started hanging out, I began to meet new people.

Although most kids were scared going into IS (intermediate school) 292, I wasn't. Tam and Sandra were a year older than me so they were already there, and I knew they would look out for me. (My birthday is in December, so I started kindergarten at four years old and was always the youngest in my class.) Freshmen at 292 were the first to get beat up or robbed. If you had some fresh kicks, a sheepskin coat, or leather bomber, you had better know someone important because if you didn't, you would be robbed.

IS 292 is where I met Latonya Jones, still my dear friend and sister today. Since Latonya and I were in the same class, we became close. Tam introduced us to her new friends and we had a nice little crew. Once Latonya took us to her godmother's house on Cleveland Street, we took things to another level.

Cleveland Street was *the* bomb! That's where we could drink, smoke weed, and just cut a fool doing any- and everything we wanted to do, like lose our virginity. Latonya's godmother, Q, was so cool. She schooled us on everything from making sure that a guy would perform oral sex on us before we gave it up, got our coochy ate before we gave it up too. *This is how you make coolies*—when you take a little of the tobacco out of a cigarette, top it with cocaine then twist the tip. Q's brother King was well known, and everybody was scared of him because he was a hardcore gang member known for robbing and beating people up. He stayed in and out of jail.

I saw a lot of violence growing up but at 13, while I was one of the 'baddest' gang-banger's girlfriend, I was introduced to new things. I thought I was all of that while I toted his guns in my book bag when he would come get me from school. He taught me so much, like how to shoot guns, carry razor blades in my mouth, and set people up. I basically did anything he said, so when it was time to ride in stolen cars looking for people he could rob, I was with it. You couldn't tell me nothing as I rocked gold chains, earrings, and rings that he stole from people. I loved me some of him, even while he cheated on me and physically abused me.

Where I grew up, it was normal for your boyfriend to hit you because they only did it because they cared. Well, my gang-banging boyfriend got locked up when I was 14. I'm 43 and he's still in jail. Once he got locked up, I already knew how to get drugs in the jail because I watched his sisters insert drugs into a balloon, stick it in their vagina, go to the bathroom during the visit, pull it out, rinse the balloon, put it in their mouth, then kiss the guy so he could swallow it. I wasn't even old enough to visit him by myself, so most of the time I used his sister's ID because she was 18. I was his ride or die for about one year. During that year, I fell in love with the street life, so even though he was locked up, I continued to live the street life.

I went to Thomas Jefferson High School, and it was a joke. By the time my crew and I got to school (about two–three hours late every day), we were already drunk and high. I got kicked out of school for truancy at 15. I was a smart girl; I just didn't like school. Since Jefferson was my neighborhood zone school, no other school accepted me. I had to wait until I was 16, then I went to Job Corp (a free residential-based education and vocational training program supported by the Department of Labor) in Laurel, MD. Tam, Rachel, and Milan our homegirl from our neighborhood joined me.

Young, pretty, fly, and being from NY, I was the at Job Corp. New Yorkers are known for being resourceful, so when I went home to visit on the weekends, they knew I would bring some weed back. Job Corp was fun. We partied, drank, and watched people trip from the effects of love boat, also known as PCP. I wasn't into coke and love boat; I only drank and smoked weed. I left Job Corp at 17 with a carpentry certificate but no GED because when it was time for me to go to school, I would cut class.

Around that time, I met another bad boy named Donny. We both were broke because he had just gotten out of jail, and I had just left Job Corp, with no job. He lived in the projects and slept on a pullout bed. When I got my $125 refund check from Job Corp, we rode the train to the Bronx, bought an eight ball of cocaine, and flipped it. Donny was one of the biggest drug dealers in the neighborhood.

Job? Please!

Once he started making money, I didn't need a job; all I had to do was be his girl, forgive him when he physically abused me, and help him with business, which meant trips to the weight spot to buy cocaine, taking it to the Dominicans to cook it, then bagging it up so it could be sold. Of course with money, cars, and drugs, women came along. After about one year of dating, we sort of broke up, but still messed around because we were so much alike: same sign, same drive. We were the clones of Bonnie and Clyde. I kept the skills I learned from him. My girls and I would still bag up for him—chop crack and stuff it in the little tubes—until our fingertips were raw. It was easy but very time-consuming. I found it easier to just be a transporter.

I went from local cabs, to out-of-state Greyhound trips, to going out of the country. Once you're known for being in that life, people spread the word. I met some Jamaicans who sent me and my friends to Jamaica, all expenses paid. Even new clothes for our trip and all the weed we could smoke while we were there. All we had to do was smuggle a suitcase each full of weed into the United States and they'd give us $2,500 each.

The first time was a piece of cake. The second time my friend Milan got locked up, so when we got to Miami and delivered the goods, we demanded that our friend come home with us. I saw my life flash before my eyes when one of my friends broke a bottle and threatened to kill the guys who came to the hotel to pay us our money. She went off, but the Jamaicans went off worse. She had a bottle and they had guns. Going back to Brooklyn knowing my friend Milan was locked up in another country was one of the hardest things I had to do. They assured us that they would pay the judge off and send her home within a week. Thank God they kept their word.

The third time I went to Jamaica to transport, I had a bad feeling because I kept thinking about the last time we went and Milan got locked up. Our four-day trip turned into ten days because the guys said the airport was unsafe, and if we went, we wouldn't get through. I cried and asked God to bring me home safe. The next day, the guys let us go home without taking any drugs with us. I promised God I would never transport again.

Well, I needed to stop messing with drugs and get a job. While in a GED program, I met Cee in a weed spot where he worked. Yep, another bad boy. I basically did every shift with him. All I had to do was be his girl, help him sell weed, forgive him when he beat me up, and he took good care of me. Clothes, jewelry, money... even a car. Oh, he also wanted me to cook for him. He was sweet at first then he was the worst, a crazy Trinidadian that had no trouble putting a 9mm in my mouth when I told him I didn't want to be with him anymore. That dude was jealous and possessive, and I was hardheaded and defiant. I was used to getting beat up by my boyfriends, so I did what I wanted to do and dealt with the consequences later. Black eyes and bruises would fade in a week; busted lips would heal in a few days.

When I got pregnant by Cee, I tried living with him, but I got tired of getting my beating and dealing with other women. I went to a homeless shelter for women so I could get a Section 8 housing voucher. I was fly as I could be while I lived in the shelter for six months, I barely stayed there, I hung with my girls all day, but had to go back to the shelter to sleep. Thank God I got an apartment before I gave birth to my son, who is now 22.

My son changed my life. His father sold drugs and lived the street life, and I knew if I continued that lifestyle, I would get locked up. When my son was about two years old, I got a job at the airport as a security officer. It didn't pay much, so I would still bag up or do local transports for extra money every now and then.

One day I realized that in order to change my life, I had to change my surroundings. I moved to Petersburg, VA, for a job as a correctional officer in 1997 and have not looked back. I left everything I knew and everyone I loved to make a new life for my son and me.

After three years as a CO (where I found out that I was an expert shooter), I decided to become a police officer. Oh my God... when I told my friends back home that I was a cop, they were like, "What the F#@^"?

I couldn't believe it myself. I failed two polygraphs on the undetected crimes portion before I found a department that didn't require a polygraph.

I moved my mom, who was sick, from New York to Virginia in 2001. She passed away in 2004. I don't have a big family and never had anyone close to me die. That was the most painful thing I ever experienced.

But when I lost my mother, I found my Father. I had no choice but to fall on my knees and ask God to help and guide me. He did exactly what I asked. I continued my career as a police officer. I was a great street cop because I came from the street. I had a special rapport with the community. I began to mentor young girls and empower them to do better. I began coordinating community events, raising money for various causes, and earned the title of special projects officer.

I've been a police officer for 15 years. I now have a beautiful family, two businesses, and I mentor for the Big Brother Big Sister program and have been with my mentee for five years. I'm also an approved foster parent, awaiting our perfect match.

You can flip your flaws just as I did.

Flaw: I stayed in the streets more than I stayed at home. Due to my reckless behavior, I wasn't very close to my mom during my teenage years. I kept her worried and didn't listen to her when she told me to stay out the streets.

Flip: In 2001, my mother took sick. After my first home purchase, I was able to bring my mother to Virginia, and I took care of her until she passed away in 2004.

Flaw: Being homeless, with the mindset: "Screw my credit. I ain't paying credit card bills. I don't need a good credit score because I'll never buy a house."

Flip: I purchased two homes when I was a single parent. Once I got married, my husband and I built our three-level home from the ground up, and we have rental properties. Yes, I'm a landlord.

Flaw: Growing up poor and not being able to go to dance school because my mom didn't have the money to pay. We stole clotheslines from people's backyards and played double-dutch on our block.

Flip: I am the owner of JumpStarz Jump Rope Lessons where we use the fun and exciting sport of double-dutch to empower youth to set and reach goals. I have a staff of 12 and have contracts with various counties, cities, organizations, and the Fort Lee military base.

Flaw: Buying, selling, and transporting drugs for large…what I thought was large amounts of money.

Flip: I learned how to extreme coupon, getting items for free, then reselling them for profit. I also own P.A.T.S. Pay and Take Stuff where I buy truckloads of liquidated furniture and resell it to the more than 1200 Facebook followers.

Flaw: Lost, not knowing my worth, being insecure, naive, used and abused in unhealthy relationships, and participating in criminal activities.

Flip: Happily married to a wonderful, hardworking, family man who has a legal job, has never put his hands on me, and is an excellent provider and father to my son and our eight-year-old daughter. I also mentor and empower young girls.

If you have flaws that you'd like to flip, here's how I flipped mine.

We all remember the five W's. Use the five W's and you can achieve anything.

Who? Who are you? I'm a strong black woman who survived domestic violence, poverty, homelessness and illegal activities. If I survived those things, I can survive anything.

What? What's your problem? Identify it! My problem was I needed to change my lifestyle.

Where? Identify where you are, now visualize where you want to be! I wanted to live a wealthy lifestyle without having to worry about going to jail.

When? When should you start? NOW! There's no perfect time. Make a plan now, set deadlines and take action.

Why? What is or who is your why? My why was my son, I knew if continued the street life, I would go to jail or be killed.

How? How can you do it? I had to leave my surroundings, this meant coming out of my comfort zone, learning new things and meeting new people. I surrounded myself with people who were at the place I wanted to be. I also began to invest in myself by attending conferences and workshops for business and personal development. I always reflect on how I got through tough situations and it reassures me that I will be fine.

No matter what walk of life you come from, we all want to flip our flaws. I invite you to take my J.U.M.P. assessment, and see if you're ready to move to a new level in life. I also have a free 30-day Jump Rope Activity log for you and your children. You can obtain these free gifts by signing up for my monthly newsletter at www.TheJumpStarz.com.

I hope my story helps someone!

No More Flaws:

Patricia's story is one of sheer strength. She reclaimed her destiny in a powerful way. She could have chosen to let her situations limit her possibility. Instead, she chose herself and flipped her flaws into an incredible woman who serves her community. She didn't allow her condition to dictate her life. It's very clear that she didn't allow her life choices be better than the power she had within herself to change her life.

The dream is free, but the hustle is going to cost you. I have discovered four things you need to do to flip your flaws and reclaim your destiny.

1. Decide to make a change and choose your goal.
2. Choose the best possible solution to move from where you are now to where you want to be. Write up a plan right now.
3. Be willing to pay the price for what you want. It is going to cost you time, energy, and money but choose to invest in yourself in all of these aspects.
4. Lastly, and the most important is, get moving and get into action.

If you want to be free, release the chains, and build a life you want to live, no matter what you have been through, your thinking must control your limitations, instead of your limitations controlling your thinking. Patricia provides a great example of that. ~Ari Squires

What do you see right now in your life? Do you see opportunity, love, happiness, success, and fulfillment?

_____

_____

_____

_____

_____

I gave examples of positive words here to keep your mind thinking forward, to uplift you, and keep you in a state of high expectations. With positive expectations, you have the power within you to overcome anything. Your expectations control your life, so it is extremely imperative that you control your expectations. If you expect the best, you will attract the BEST. I call that your inner manifestation magnet. Look forward to your future with positive expectations and then get excited about it! Enthusiasm is a powerful motivating force and one of the greatest secrets to your success! ~Ari Squires

About T.F. Sterling

T.F. Sterling is a certified holistic fitness coach, nutritionist, and personal trainer with more than 8 years' experience in the health and fitness industry. Her own journey from being overweight and unhealthy, to being healthy and fit helped her realize that it's not only about dieting or restrictive eating habits. It's about looking within and becoming aware of the thoughts and emotions that cause self-sabotage and emotional eating. This gives her the ability to work with her clients in a non-judgmental way. Transformation begins with changing your mindset, taking action, and committing to the process daily. Her story was featured on the Black Women Losing Weight website as "Transformation of the Day" on January 1, 2016.

She truly believes that when you make a decision with a firm belief, the right people will show up and doors will open. She believes that every day is a new opportunity for something good to happen, even when things seem their worst. Find your *power why*. She calls it that because it has to be a reason so powerful that it drives you to succeed against all odds. Her two sons are her power why. They are everything to her, and she is determined to make them proud and show them by example that no matter what happens to you, or what others say about you, you have the power to accomplish whatever you set out to do.

Chapter 8

From Fear to Freedom

T.F. STERLING

--◦◦◦◦◦◦◦◦--

Every one of us is called upon, perhaps many times, to start a new life. A frightening diagnosis, a marriage, (a divorce), a move, loss of a job, ...And onward full-tilt we go, pitched and wrecked and absurdly resolute, driven in spite of everything to make good on a new shore. To be hopeful, to embrace one possibility after another--that is surely the basic instinct...Crying out: High tide! Time to move out into the glorious debris. Time to take this life for what it is.
~Barbara Kingsolver

As we pulled out of the driveway with a few pieces of essential furniture and the things that were of personal value to me, I looked back and realized that I was about to embark on a new life. My emotions ranged from relief and triumph to a little anxiety. I was driving away from a 25-year marriage, a beautiful home, a lucrative business, and all the dreams and plans I had made for a future. I left it all behind. My teenage son and I were about to start a new life that would be quite different from the one we had known.

I had been married to a military man. We were both in our early 20's on active duty when we met and married after knowing each other for only six months. Shortly after, I left the military to travel with him and start a family. Three years into the marriage, our first son came along, and we bought our first home. Life was wonderful. Then the inevitable happened. He got a three-year assignment with a unit that would rotate between the US and South Pacific. I didn't want to live alone with a baby for three years, so I went home to the Virgin Islands to be with my family.

Eventually, I moved back to the US to be with him. Three years of separation can put a strain on any marriage. My husband was becoming a stranger to me. I found letters indicating he'd been having an affair, and I was devastated. I forgave him and tried to make life seem normal even though his assignments kept him gone most of the time. We had been married nine years when our second son came along.

As the years went by, I made so many sacrifices, including not having a career of my own, so that he could have a successful military career. Thirteen moves in 20 years, and through it all, I was there taking care of our two sons. I put up with the long separations and focused on holding the family together by being a supportive wife and mother.

> *When we choose to be what others want us to be, we end up being dissatisfied with our life, because we are not living from our authenticity, but from our domestication.*
> *~Heather Ash Amara*

Life has a funny way of bringing things to light. We can choose to ignore the painful signs and try to be the perfect wife and mother, painting a beautiful picture for the world to see, while all the time miserable inside. That was my life. For many years, it was like a rollercoaster ride. The highs of traveling and living in different countries, nice vacations, and the lows of being virtually a single parent raising our two sons, feeling unloved and unappreciated.

Our final assignment was in Cote D'Ivoire, Africa. It was wonderful to be there. We made the best of it. We made new friends, traveled to Ghana, and had a great experience overall.

Then it happened.

In December 1999, the Ivorian military overthrew the government. We were in a state of emergency, and my sons and I were alone. He was stranded in Liberia. I saw things you would only see on TV: dead bodies on the street, soldiers with guns shooting randomly and stealing cars. I had no choice but to be strong for my sons. Eventually, when things calmed down after a few months we came back to the US.

Normal didn't last long for me. Infidelity reared its ugly head again. I found detailed emails between them. *How could he do this??* After everything that we had just gone through. I was devastated. I called him and asked why. His response was like a knife in my heart. He said I wasn't woman enough, and I was fat and ugly.

I just cried. Yes, I was overweight. Over the years, I had let myself go. I had gained about 50 pounds. At my annual checkup, my doctor told me I was pre-diabetic and my cholesterol was high. He strongly advised me to lose weight. I was very unhappy with myself and my life. I began dieting to feel better about myself. Nothing worked and every failure left me feeling worse, but I kept up the façade of the happy wife, not realizing it wasn't really about food.

He came home, and once again, I forgave him in hopes that things would be different. We bought a home in Northern Virginia, and things seemed good for a while, I decided to start my own business, specializing in custom drapery. Sewing beautiful fabrics and decorating made me happy. My business was doing very well. I was finally beginning to feel successful at something. I remember the first check I got. After a one-hour consultation, I walked away with a $2,000 down payment. I was beyond excited!

A few days later while we were at dinner with friends, I was telling them about my business and that I had my first client.

He commented, "Yeah, when she told me she was going to make drapery, I didn't think anything would come of it."

I was shocked and disappointed by his comment. He really didn't believe in me. He didn't seem to want me to be successful.

I had been saving money to buy a van for my company. When he learned of this he got angry and yelled, "Why do you have all that money in your account?"

I tried to explain that I was going to buy a van for the business. He continued to be upset, and once again, I gave in to his wishes. I didn't buy the van. I was afraid to make him angrier. Whenever he raised his voice, it would take me back to my childhood, and I would feel the same fear I felt when my father abused my mother. I never realized how much this impacted my life.

As my business continued to grow, so did his resentment. I tried to involve him in the business hoping he'd be more agreeable, but he had a habit of putting me down in front of my customers and sometimes becoming confrontational.

I began going to conferences and meeting other people in the design industry. My business was growing and the future looked bright. Little did I know that feeling wasn't going to last.

The final straw for me came after he had hip surgery, when his mom and I walked into his hospital room and came face-to-face with the other woman. I didn't say a word. I didn't want a scene. He was just lying there looking foolish. He murmured some introductions, and I knew for sure. So, there we were in his hospital room. It got uncomfortable and she decided to leave. I followed her out and his mom confronted her. As I stood there, feeling humiliated, his mom began to threaten her, and she left. It was an awful scene that I will never forget.

When he finally came home from the hospital, I asked for a divorce.

He laughed in my face and said, "You're not going anywhere."

"Just wait and see."

At that moment, he raised one of the crutches to hit me. I dodged and ran. As I opened the front door, he reached out, pushed me, and slammed the door saying, "Get out of my house!"

This wasn't the first time he had pushed me, and I reached my breaking point. I showed up the next day with a police escort, took some of our things, and my son and I went to stay with friends.

I had been seeing a counselor for a few months. My doctor prescribed depression medication that made me feel sick all the time. I decided to stop taking it and started doing things that actually made me happy. I took a belly dance class. I love music, and I love to dance. Belly dance was new for me, and I loved it. It really helped me to begin loving myself.

I also joined a book club with a friend. It felt good to be around positive women and read great books. We got dressed up for our monthly meetings, we laughed, we cried, and we had great times. Even when you are going through a storm, it helps to surround yourself with positive energy, pick yourself up, dress up, and show up. Find the things that you love to do, the things that bring true joy to your spirit.

My counselor eventually referred me to ACTS (Action in Community Through Service) a non-profit organization that has a domestic violence intervention program and provides a safe house for women attempting to leave abusive relationships. There were so many women there with similar stories. It helped to know that I wasn't alone. Emotional abuse is often worse than physical abuse. It's so insidious that most women don't recognize it until it escalates to physical abuse. After a few weeks of meetings, I decided to go back home. Everyone thought I was crazy, but I had a plan. I needed to get the finances in order. I had taken full advantage of the free resources that were available and made a step-by-step plan. I spent hours doing research and reading everything about military divorce cases. I was determined to get out of the marriage with all that I was entitled to.

I read *Listen to Your Life* by Valorie Burton. That book set me on the path to self-discovery. But the book that had the most impact then was Burton's *What's Really Holding You Back?* I didn't just read the book and put it away. I did the worksheets, and I kept a journal. I realized that fear was the driving force in my life. Fear was the chain that kept me in an emotionally abusive marriage for 25 years. Fear that began as a child when I saw my father regularly abuse my mother physically and emotionally. It kept me from speaking up for myself. It chipped away at my self-esteem.

A counselor recommended the book *Do It Afraid* by Joyce Meyer. It helped me to understand that the key to overcoming your fears is to keep moving through those doors even when you feel afraid. Each time you step forward, you build your confidence to keep going. Start small; try something you have always wanted to do. You eventually realize that you can overcome the obstacles.

I was becoming a different person. I had a plan and I felt empowered. I knew leaving wouldn't be easy, and I feared he would become confrontational or even violent. I was able to recognize those thoughts as that fear from my childhood rearing its ugly head again. I began to use meditation to acknowledge the negative thought pattern and then create a positive, empowering statement.

Here is an example. *Even though I feel afraid that he will be confrontational and violent, I choose to let go of my fears and focus on how I can safely get away. I have a plan and I know that it will all work out in a way that's right for me.*

I repeated this in the morning and at night. It did work out for me. He got a work assignment in South America. I had a whole week to pack what I needed and leave. I rented a U-Haul, called some friends, and made arrangements. With their help, I was able to pack the truck in a few hours. As we pulled out of the driveway, I wished I could see the look on his face when he returned. He thought I was weak, but I had found my strength.

You can too!

His refusal to pay child support put a real strain on my finances, but I held on. It took two years before the divorce was final. Walking out of that courtroom, I felt finally free. My sons and I moved to Orlando a few weeks later.

I had closed my business. The legal fees had taken a toll on my finances and ruined my credit. When things got really bad, I sold my jewelry and wedding rings to buy food. Bills kept piling up, creditors kept calling, and I was in a constant state of anxiety that my car would be repossessed. One day I came home to find the power had been turned off. I just sat there and cried. I couldn't believe this was happening to me. I was able to work out a payment plan. Thank goodness!

I had begun a popular diet program and lost 50 pounds in about eight months. This time it was more for health reasons. I wanted to avoid taking medication. I was feeling a lot better about myself. I was more in control of my life. I really wanted to stay healthy, so I began walking on the treadmill at the gym every morning.

I'm not a runner, and I don't like running was my mantra. But as time went on, I decided to give it a try. I would walk for six minutes then run for one minute. Week by week, I increased my run time and decreased the walk time. Eventually, I found I could run three to four miles every day. It gave me such a sense of accomplishment, I felt energized, stronger, and more confident despite all that was going on in my life. I realized that old belief had been holding me back. I wasn't dieting anymore either. By releasing what had been weighing me down—unworthiness, depression, fear, emotional abuse—I released the weight I'd been struggling with for years. I was no longer in a struggle. I had been focusing on the symptom and not the core issue.

Reading personal development books helped me to get through the tough times. My favorite quote by Wayne Dyer *When you change the way you look at things, the things you look at change*, helped me realize how my thoughts shaped my reality. We can shift our thoughts to create more positive outcomes in our life. As I became more aware of the negative thought patterns and words that were rooted in my childhood, I started looking at who they came from and why. I realized that a lot of the beliefs I had were from people with a less evolved way of thinking. Therefore, they were not valid.

> *Your doubts are not a product of accurate thinking, but habitual thinking. Years ago, you accepted flawed conclusions as correct and began to live your life as if those warped ideas about your potential were true, and ceased the bold experiment in living.... Now it's time to find that faith you had in yourself before. ~ Price Pritchet*

Through my journey and transformation, I found my purpose. I had gone from being overweight, depressed, feeling unloved, unworthy, and fearful, to feeling stronger, more confident, and being fit and healthy without medication. I am now a certified holistic fitness coach. I believe in taking a mind-body approach to health, fitness, and personal growth. My mission is to empower women who struggle with weight to overcome limiting beliefs and emotional eating so that they can be more confident, have more energy, and look and feel amazing for good. Everyone has a story based on beliefs about themselves and their abilities. Often these subconscious beliefs and emotions are the driving force keeping you from accomplishing your goals.

To overcome these beliefs and negative emotions, I began a consistent guided meditation practice. The power to transform your life is within you. That voice deep within always tells the truth. Meditation helps you tap into those negative, subconscious thoughts and begin to shift those thoughts to more positive ones. If you are a beginner, I suggest guided meditation to help keep you centered and focused.

Here are a few tips to begin transforming your life:
- Take time to listen to the voice deep inside. Why are you emotionally eating?
- Challenge the beliefs about yourself and the weight loss ideas that were given to you by your mother, your friends, the media. Just because something is said to be right doesn't mean that it is.
- Invest in yourself. It's okay to start thinking you are worthy. Your feelings and well-being can be a priority. Your health and happiness is important, and it is a good thing to take action to achieve what you want.
- Try something new. We tend to be creatures of habit. We continuously do the same things expecting a different result. Try something you never thought you could do. You don't have to settle for things as they are. It's time to try something new.

You know you deserve more in life. You deserve to be more confident and have more energy. You deserve to have the healthy, fit body you envision so that you can look fabulous in anything you choose. I am proof that it can be done. I want to inspire you to live your best life *now*.

To help you change your mind and change your body, I've created this free five-day video training to provide you with the tools you need to begin your journey to being more confident, healthy, and fit with less effort and more fun.

https://sterlingtotalfitness.com/change-your-mind-change-your-body/

For me, succeeding against the odds meant losing everything, all my hopes and plans for a future, and still having the courage and strength to pick myself up, examine my old thoughts and beliefs, and connect with myself and the power that lies within me to change direction and create a new life that's even more rewarding than before. It meant being able let go of things and people that kept me locked in a place of pain. I now have a consistent meditation practice that has helped me to become more conscious of my thoughts and how they create my reality. A whole new world of possibility has opened for me.

My biggest hope for humanity is for all to understand the power that we have within us to change our lives and to change how we relate to each other. We can only change the world by first transforming our own lives.

> *Change is inevitable, but transformation is by conscious choice. While you do not always have control over how or when the changes will occur in your life, you can choose how you are in relation to those changes. When you step towards rather than ignore, fight, or resist change, you reclaim your personal freedom. You step onto a path of transformation, and move from being a victim of change to being a co-creator with change. ~ Heather Ash Amara, Warrior Goddess Training*

Recommended Books for Mental Transformation:
   Warrior Goddess Training, Heather Ash Amara
   Excuses Be Gone, Wayne Dyer
   Listen to Your Life, Valorie Burton
   What's Really Holding You Back, Valorie Burton
   The Four Agreements, Don Miguel Ruiz
   The Alchemist, Paolo Coelho
   Breaking the Habit of Being Yourself: How to Lose Your Mind and Create a New One, Dr. Joe Dispenza

No More Fear:

This is a moving story of slapping fear in the face and taking your life back! Pema Chödrön says that "Fear is a natural reaction to moving closer to the truth". T.F's determination to prevail sure proves that. She had to tap into her fears and see where her limiting beliefs about herself were showing up. She could have blamed her husband, but instead she did the necessary work required to create more self-awareness.

Many of us like to avoid looking at ourselves this honestly. It is it much easier to suppress things or hide from them. But until we look at it, we cannot change it.

Many of us also make our fear 'wrong' and try to run away from it, as though it is some dark part of ourselves that we should be ashamed of.

But I am going to encourage you to look at it head on – square in the face.

As you start this process, things may get uncomfortable, but that is ok, just breathe through it. Do not beat up on yourself. Do not be hard on yourself. Just notice what is going on in your mind without attachment.

Fear will play out as self-doubt. It will play out through negative thinking. It plays out when we tear other people down.

You are not your fear. ~Ari Squires

Witnessing Your Fear Exercise:

What are some fearful thoughts you find yourself often thinking?

_____

_____

_____

_____

_____

What happens in your body when you think these thoughts? How does it make you feel? Where in your body does it sit? Does it have a color, shape, size or texture? Start to really connect and become familiar with this fear.

_____

_____

_____

_____

_____

What are the triggers that cause these fearful thoughts to start playing in your mind? What typically starts the pattern?

_____

_____

_____

_____

_____

What are the stories you have created around these thoughts eg: If you feel you are not good enough, what have you made this mean that you feel you cannot do in your life?

_____

_____

_____

_____

_____

How is Fear Driving You?:
How do your fears drive your actions, behavior and decisions?

_____

_____

_____

_____

_____

Where in your life do you project these fears on to others?

_____

_____

_____

_____

How are these fears holding you back and keeping you small?

_____

_____

_____

_____

If these fears were actually serving the purpose of keeping you safe, what would they be keeping you safe from? How are these fears protecting you?

_____

_____

_____

_____

Sitting with Your Fear Exercise:

How often do you push down your emotions or try to run from them in an attempt to not have to feel them? What is your typical response when you feel something – is it to grab something to eat, to turn the TV on to distract yourself, or to keep yourself busy so you don't have to feel ii?

If you do any of these, I want you to start to connect with and *feel* your emotions.

This process will be uncomfortable. But is the only way to process and release what you are feeling. If you don't allow the energy inside of you to be expressed in some way, it will remain bottled up inside of you and will eventually be triggered in an unresourceful way.

So, next time you feel the discomfort of an unpleasant emotion, I want you to practice the following.

Stop what you are doing and take a moment to sit still and close your eyes. (When I used to work in a day job, I would actually go in to the bathroom and lock myself in there for 5 minutes so I could practice this.)

Tune in to your body and notice the physical sensations that the emotion is creating. Where is it sitting in your body?

Focus in on it even more and start to really allow yourself to feel the feeling

Then accept the feeling. Open up to it. Begin to welcome it in and create even more space for it to be expressed. Keep tuning in to it and feeling it.

Try not to analyze or think about the feeling. But rather, stay in your body and stay with the sensations you are experiencing. If your mind wanders, keep bringing it back to the feeling.

Surrender to the energy that is surging up inside of you and allow it to be expressed. Sometimes you may just feel the energy shift and move into a different sensation, or other times you will have the desire to express the emotion in some way. If you feel that way, allow it to come out.

Continue sitting with that feeling and do not go and do anything else until you have felt it transform or disappear.

Chains Converted as Inner Strength

Artwork by Seo Yong-Deon

www.liquidartsysem.com

Every great dream begins with a dreamer. Always remember, you have within you the strength, the patience, and the passion to reach for the stars to change the world.
~Harriet Tubman

About Ari Squires

Ari Squires organically serves as an authentic living life coach, business trainer, and speaker who guides entrepreneurs to discover a new way of living - a way that is free from struggle, fear and limitation and is filled to the brim with freedom, peace and abundance of everything you love.

Through her life-changing online programs, sold out workshops and seminars, 1:1 mentoring and mastermind groups she is opening the hearts and minds of hundreds of people from all over the country to release their chains.

Chapter 9

Your Power Within to Tap into Your Inner G

ARI SQUIRES

◦◦◦◦◦◦◦◦

We have all experienced those turning points in our lives. The moments when a decision changes everything. Where we know, right then and there, we are redefining ourselves and shifting the course of our life.

These opportunities often fill us with overwhelming inner conflict. One voice pushes us back into the security of our comfort zone while another voice pulls us forward so powerfully that we simply cannot say no.

We can either keep cruising on the same old track, or we can forge our own trail. We can redefine our future and write a brand-new script for our life.

These are the moments where one decision changes everything. These are our daring moments, where we teeter on the edge of fear. Where life dares us to take the leap.

Say yes or say no.

Act on your heart or listen to fear.

Stay or walk away.

Step up or keep hiding.

An opportunity presents itself. We feel the pull. But we falter. We hesitate. We step back. We take time to think. We over-analyze. We worry.

When all we need to do is just stand in our power and say yes.

It is in these moments that life calls you out: *So, what's it going to be? Are you gonna keep playing that same game you've always played, or are you going to do something different? Are you going to step up? Are you going to say yes?*

Life is like: *Well, here's your chance. Show me what the hell you've got.*

What do you do?

The Chain Releasing Moments That Changed My Life

I have experienced many of these dramatic shifts over the past few years. My daring moments have been turning points, where I have made heart-driven decisions that changed the course of my entire life.

November 13, 2009

I will never forget the day I hit publish on my first ever Facebook post. I was terrified. The idea of having my innermost thoughts and feelings live on the Internet for all to see seemed crazy. Back then, it was still new to share your life on social media, and people asked me why on earth I would want to share myself so publicly.

But I had a deep, powerful message I had been holding inside that I wanted to share with the world. It was a message that had been sitting inside of me for way too long. It was time to be seen. The desire to give my words a public platform became stronger and more powerful than the fear I felt. And so I did it. My journey of releasing my chains began on that day and has now continued for the past seven years and has turned into a national movement.

July 29, 2013

This was the day I signed for up my business coach training. It was the day I finally said yes to the desire that had been burning within me for nine years. It was the day I finally found the courage to follow my heart.

I was on the phone with my coach, palms all sweaty and adrenalin pumping through my body. I had been deliberating on making this bold move for six months, and I simply couldn't delay it any longer. The conversation was a blur. I gave her my credit card details and locked myself in. I got off the phone shaking. I knew I had made a decision that would change my life forever.

June 20, 2014

I had been waiting months for this day. After ten years operating my terribly stressful but highly profitable dance and performing arts school, I was moving on. I had been in a hectic transition period for most of the year, trying to juggle the school, a part-time coaching business, and my duties as a loving wife and mom. And now my moment had arrived. I could finally spend every single day doing the work that I was born to do.

As I shared my journey with my tribe on social media, people asked me what I was planning on doing. All I could say was: *I don't know.* I had a few part-time clients, $1000 in my savings account and no plan. But I knew I was doing the right thing. I showed up so fully for that journey, and within six weeks, I had a full-time load of coaching clients and had launched AriSquires.com. I have never felt so scared in my whole life, yet at the same time, I have never felt so spiritually supported, free, and guided by my Source either.

Nothing Happens Until You Decide

All these moments have been transformative for me. One decision has quite simply changed the course of my life.

When you stand on the edge of these chain-releasing moments, you don't need to know what is going to happen. You don't need to know how it is going to unfold. All you need to do is say yes.

Nothing happens until you decide. The money you need will not show up. The opportunities will not present themselves. Not a single shift will occur. You have to decide first.

> *"Until one is committed, there is hesitancy, the chance to draw back – Concerning all acts of initiative (and creation), there is one elementary truth that ignorance of which kills countless ideas and splendid plans: that the moment one definitely commits oneself, then Providence moves too. All sorts of things occur to help one that would never otherwise have occurred. A whole stream of events issues from the decision, raising in one's favor all manner of unforeseen incidents, meetings and material assistance, which no man could have dreamed would come his way. Whatever you can do, or dream you can do, begin it. Boldness has genius, power, and magic in it. Begin it now".* –Goethe

Change Happens the Minute You Say Yes to What Your Heart Is Calling You Toward

There is a common theme that has run through each of those turning points: I made the decision to follow my heart. I chose to act on what I loved rather than let the voice of fear rule me. I chose to believe in a new possibility, rather than my programming of generational fear.

In each of those life-changing situations, I had been so bound with fear that I could barely breathe. But below the fear was another energy. I call this my *inner G*—my inner greatness, inner God, and inner gangsta—that only sees and knows possibility. My inner G was calm, encouraging, and powerful. It was the energy of my heart telling me that the step I was about to take was perfect, aligned, and the right thing I could do.

In each of those moments, I felt that the love I had for what I wanted, and the desire I had to express my truth, was more powerful than my fear. It pushed me beyond all limitations.

The voice of love was calling me—no, it was shaking me by the shoulders telling me to wake up! Calling me to expand, to grow, and to become more. It tugged at me. It stretched me. And when I listened to it and trusted it whole-heartedly, it propelled me beyond my fear.

Choose Love Energy or Succumb to Fear Energy; What's It Going to Be?

In every moment, you are choosing which energy will rule your life. Fear energy will cause you to withdraw, shrink, hesitate, hide, and say no. Love (your inner G) energy will call you to step out, expand, decide, be seen, and say yes.

You can choose. Be dominated by fear, or be lifted by your inner G. It's up to you.

The only way I could make the decisions I did was by going deeper into myself to listen, to feel, to tune into my inner guidance that lays deep below my mind that wants to control everything. I made that deep, inner, loving voice, more real than the fear-driven voice of my mind.

In each of those moments, I could have chosen to believe in fear more than my faith. To buy into the limitation. To let it stop me. But

I made a different choice. I chose love. I chose to do what I loved. I chose to listen to the loving voice. I tapped into the power within me, my inner G, and I chose to say yes to my heart.

Was it easy? No. Was I petrified? Yes. But did I feel the most alive than I have ever felt in my entire life? Abso-freaking-lutely. It was magic!

And this will be your daring moment. The moment when you decide to say yes to your heart, to follow what you love and do something different. The moment when you choose to stop hesitating, avoiding, and procrastinating. The moment you show up fully for what you want. The moment you act in the face of fear. The moment you release your chains and say yes to you.

Personifying Your Highest Self

See, we're all going about change backward. We're going about it the wrong way. If any of you reading know there are changes you need to make, it's not about changing things on the outside: home, body, cars, more money. It's about embodying a different inner G.

How do you do that?

The shift begins the moment you change your energy, change your being. It's about changing how you're feeling and how you're feeling about yourself.

I ran so many times—from creating this No More Chains Movement, from videos, from showing up visibly in my business. But at this moment as I'm sitting here—connected to a feeling of complete worthiness and honoring of my value, my worth, my skills, my gifts, my talents, and my divinity—writing this message to you is the most effortless thing in the world. I'm not even trying. I'm just simply feeling connected to the love of who I am. And from that place I naturally feel inspired and moved to share it.

When you connect to the love of who you are, you will naturally feel inspired and move to nourish your body with good foods. You will naturally want to take care of yourself. You're also naturally drawn to people who love and care for you. You'll naturally find yourself in fulfilling situations because that's the energy you attract. Like metal to a magnet. That is what's driving everything that you're doing.

I know this can be challenging because many of us, including myself, were not taught how to tap into our power within. I can imagine that some of you are thinking: *Wow. How do we begin making this shift in our energy and tap into our inner G?*

It's easy now for me in my morning meditation practice, where I choose to access a different energy beyond the energy of my limited mind. It's when I choose to create some space and stop reacting phonetically to the voice in my head that is constantly barking orders at me and telling me all the things I need to do. I let that go; I let that be there. And I begin to notice which energy is driving me every moment.

In those moments, I ask myself if I'm responding and reacting to a fearful, limiting voice that is telling me I'm insignificant, unworthy, and incapable of having what I want. If that's going on, I'm not going to act on it. I'm going to stop, pause, breathe inward, and tune in within. I'm going to choose to draw my attention into my energy of love and what it would feel like to be my higher self and tune into the energy of my higher self. I just sit with that for a while, and I breathe into the feeling of worthiness, deserving, self-honoring and abundance, and knowing that I am magnificent and just feel that energy. And then I ask what action I should take today, how to move forward.

It's moment-by-moment as you tap into your power within. Love then guides you to different actions from what you would normally do. It guides you to your highest potential. It guides you onto the highest path. And that's when your outer world and opportunities start to change. By choosing to spend time each day honoring your worth and your magnificence—It doesn't have to be in the morning; you can do it at any time—and then letting that energy guide your life, all your dreams are going to manifest.

I had to take a lot of big action over the years to bring what I wanted to life. And I know this next chapter and the next vision for the No More Chains Movement will also require a lot of action, will be scary, and will be outside my comfort zone.

I want you to be aware of what is driving your action. The energy behind your action. Focus on who you are being. What energy are you aligned with? Are you embodying some negative energy that is causing you to be scared, limited, unsure, unworthy, and powerless? Is your mind telling you to respond from a place of reaction, control, and overthinking? Or are you embodying and connecting to the energy of your higher self? If you simply surrender to the energy of your higher self—which feels worthy, whole, complete, abundant, and knows that you're capable of anything—that will guide you moment by moment. This is what you were born for. Know that your heart never gives you desires unless they are possible.

That's that first step of tuning into and getting connected with that power within you, and then the action piece is asking that energy to guide your actions.

What are the actions that I can take today?

What inspired the action?

Is there someone I need to contact?

Is there something I need to do?

Do I need to act in a different way in the scenario that is going to play out today?

Do I need to change how I'm handling my finances?

Do I need to change how I'm handling a relationship?

Let the action that you take be driven from the wholeness of your higher being, not from your limited, chained self.

Wow, I felt really different when I sent that email ... made that call ... did that presentation ... wrote that blog post.

As the result of taking different actions, you will create different results, and seeing that is the cool part.

Look how differently the world responded. Look at the different feedback. Look at the synchronicity that opened up. Look at the way that relationship healed or transformed. Look at that opportunity that just dropped in your inbox. Look at the response you get to the blog post you wrote. Look at how the job you wanted just dropped into your lap.

So it begins with the state of being; it flows into love-driven and love-inspired action; and then it manifests different physical results. Just remember: you can't skip the inner work. That is what I wanted to start here. The inner work is where the true transformation begins and ends. That's what connects every chapter in this book.

And if you're ever overwhelmed or stuck, it's most likely because you're in a state of fear. Let that fear go. My favorite author, Napoleon Hill, says: "When you are faced with your own 'emergency', fear can either motivate you or paralyze you. By recognizing that you have a choice and reacting positively to your fears, you can permanently change your life for the better."

Come back to you, align your energy to a state of power, and then move forward from there—not knowing how everything is going to come together but knowing you feel different. You show up different. You act differently. Then the pieces of the puzzle start to come together. Your story line starts to shift, opportunities emerge, the money arrives, circumstances change, and your dreams start to come true.

You've witnessed that as you are enjoying the stories of these amazing women who have let go of their generational scars and curses and are blazing a new trail by writing their stories.

No More Chains Success Kit

If you want to get more connected to your power within, visit www.NoMoreChainsSuccessKit.com to download a free kit that allows you to reach deep down inside yourself to pull out your inner G. You can't achieve any high level of success without releasing your chains and that takes a special type of power. The kit includes *The Inner G Transformation Guide*, which helps you pull back the layers to tap into your super powers; an audio course on the *Six Signs You're in Transformation*; and the *Mindset, Money & Motivation: Wealth Conscious Manifestation* video course. If implemented consistently, these tools will lead you to No More Chains, so you can create the life and business that you love.

My hope is that you no longer look to the outside world for change, but instead look inside. You have the power within you to release your chains.

No More Giving Your Power Away:

"Change the way you look at things and the things you look at change." Wayne W. Dyer

Perception is Projection

What does 'perception is projection' mean? It means - we don't see things as they are. We see them as *we* are. The way we perceive the world, determines the world we project around us. This means having the ability to change the reality we are projecting, simply by changing how we are seeing it.

Everything, every event, every person is neutral. It just is. And then we come along and we place a label on it. We label it as good or bad, right or wrong, positive or negative. We also make it mean something.

Your true power lies in not necessarily changing your reality, but in changing the way you are experiencing your reality – changing the way you are labelling the events, people or circumstances in your life. And most importantly, changing what you are making these events mean about YOU.

The way we perceive the world is based on our beliefs, our memories, our thoughts and our emotions. These all combine together to create our 'stories'. Our stories are the chain of thoughts that typically play through our minds about the different areas of our lives.

The problem is that many of us have come to believe that our stories are true! We have spent our whole life accruing evidence from our world to support them. Because we have been perceiving the world through our stories, we have in turn created a world that reflects our stories.

Once you realize that everything you're telling yourself is just a story, you now have a choice. You can choose how you perceive your world. You can choose to perceive your world in a way that supports and empowers you rather than in a way that limits and disempowers you.

What is Your Story?:

Think about the following 4 different areas of your life. What are the stories you tell yourself about what is possible for you in these areas? What are the core beliefs you have? What experiences from the past do you play on repeat in your mind? What thoughts do you generally think about each?

Career:

_____

_____

_____

_____

_____

Relationships:

_____

_____

_____

_____

_____

Finances:

_____

_____

_____

_____

_____

Body/Health:

_____

_____

_____

_____

_____

Re-Write Your Story:

What if you could choose a new story? What would you create? What would you like to believe? What new story could you write in each area that would empower you, support you and take you to where you want to go? Write them below.

Career:

_____

_____

_____

_____

_____

Relationships:

_____

_____

_____

_____

_____

Finances:

_____

_____

_____

_____

_____

Body/Health:

_____

_____

_____

_____

Visualize Your New Reality:

Read over the new stories you wrote on the previous pages. Think about how you would feel if you lived from those stories. Who would you be? What would be possible for you? What would you be doing? What would you look like?

Close your eyes and start to let your imagination run wild.
Begin to visualize what your life would look like if those stories formed your reality.
What would your career be like?
What would your relationships be like?
What would your finances be like?
What would your body and your state of health be like?
Picture it all on the screen of your mind with crystal clear clarity. Play it like a movie where you are the main character.
Feel the feelings of what it would be like to be living these new stories.
Keep seeing the pictures in your mind and experiencing the details of your life.
Continue with this exercise until you begin to feel that what you are seeing on the screen of your mind is real.

Remember, we co-create in our life, whatever it is that we think about most. So, keep thinking these new thoughts, visualizing this new way of living, and feelings these new feelings and soon this will start to become your reality.

About Rhonda Watts-Robinson

Minister Rhonda Watts-Robinson, also known as "The Greatness Igniter", is a life-changing International Speaker, Certified Life and Business Coach, Minister, and Educator whose purpose and passion is to daily transform women's lives, their businesses, and assist them in elevating in their God-ordained purpose. She is the epitome of a young woman after God's own heart who consistently operates in her unique gifts and talents.

In 2003, Minister Rhonda obtained her English and Education Degree from the University of Massachusetts-Dartmouth. In 2011, Min. Rhonda graduated Cum Laude from The Samuel Dewitt Proctor School of Theology with her Masters of Divinity Degree. Prior to this, she was licensed to preach the gospel in 2005 and has been preaching on the battle for the Lord ever since.

Minister Rhonda has traveled both nationally and internationally speaking and teaching transformation and spiritual elevation. She has traveled on various mission trips around the world where she has had the opportunity to display the love of Jesus Christ to those around her.

Rhonda is also a passionate entrepreneur and owner of two successful online businesses, Reap Your Abundance, LLC and Rhonda's Writing Services, as well as the founder of The "Sisters Elevating Success" Institute, which is an online institute for the Christ-Centered woman who is ready to elevate in her business, life, ministry, and relationship with Jesus Christ. Along with this, Rhonda is also the founder of Rhonda Watts-Robinson's International Ministries.

Minister Rhonda is the proud mother of three beautiful babies and best friend to her husband of five years. It is her passion to assist others in elevating and experiencing abundance and reaching their next level of God-ordained greatness.

Minister Rhonda Watts-Robinson lives by the words of her favorite scripture found in John 4:34: *"My food, said Jesus, "is to do the will of him who sent me and to finish his work."*

Chapter 10

The Deliverance Behind Your Diagnosis

RHONDA WATTS-ROBINSON

-◦◦◦◦◦◦◦◦-

Have you ever been put in a situation where your life literally flashed before your eyes? Have you ever gone through a traumatic experience that changed your life in the blink of an eye? Have you ever been diagnosed with an illness or disease that had the ability to impact the whole essence of who you are and made you question everything you believe? Have you ever been given news that caused you to question how much longer you had to live and if life would even be worth living anymore?

If you have answered "yes" to any of the above questions, you, my friend, have an understanding of what I once felt at a point in my life. I remember the experience like it was yesterday. I went to the doctor's office for what I thought was a routine checkup after coming back from Africa on a year-long missionary trip. It was just another average day in my book. I was grateful to be alive, to have my family, and for the many blessings God had bestowed upon me as His child. I was a minister of the Gospel and a young woman at the ripe age of 24 with an anointed calling in life. Yes, I was aware of all of this. Yes, I was aware of all that God had in store for me. But on this day, a cold day in the month of November 2004, my life completely changed.

As I sat in the doctor's office and the female physician walked back in with my test results; I admit, I wasn't prepared for the news that was about to impact my entire life. I had walked through the doors of my doctor's office on this day to receive what I thought would be a routine checkup, but this day inevitably became the day that tested and tried the whole target of my life, my essence of being, my beliefs, and my world. As the doctor stood over me, she proceeded to tell me the horrifying news that changed my life forever:

"Hello, Rhonda. Well, all of your results have come back… and they all looked good and came back negative – all except for one result…" It was then that there was a pause in the small, closed-door cubicle called a doctor's office. As she took a deep breath, she proceeded to say the seven words I will never forget for the rest of my days: "Rhonda, your HIV test came back positive."

There was a silence… a silence that I'm sure was short, but yet seemed so very long because, in that moment, in that instant, my life literally flashed before my eyes.

What the doctor was thinking as she looked back at me with no emotion after telling me this news, I had no idea. Honestly, when I heard those words; I didn't care. In that moment, I felt a heightened rush of every negative emotion overtake me: overwhelming fear, regret, confusion, anger, failure; an uncertainty of what my remaining days called life would bring me.

I looked back at her and all I could muster up to ask was, "Am I going to live or am I going to die?" Her response was the icing on the cake that led me down the road of destruction and confusion. "Well, we are going to have to refer you to a specialist. I don't feel I can discuss this with you right now"

This happened over twelve years ago. Yep, twelve years ago, my life flashed before my eyes. Twelve years ago, I was diagnosed HIV Positive.

Unbeknownst to me at the time, I slowly began to allow the chains of fear, lack of self-esteem, and self-worth to set up shop within my mind. Along with this, although I was a minister of the gospel, I allowed my full faith in God's word and healing power to plummet to nearly being nonexistent in regards to this situation – this test in my life. I admit, I was a Minister Hemmed in Chains!

What would people say?

What would people think?

Would I even live and make it to truly fulfill the purpose, the visions, the legacy, and the calling God had placed in my heart?

Would I soon become sick?

Would my loved ones have to see me suffer?

Would I ever have a man truly love me with my condition?

Would I ever have children and, if I did, would they be healthy?

Did I disappoint God?

Did I mess up my calling?

After being told this news, I specifically remember my ride home that day. I was alone in my car, but I also felt alone within. I remember crying out to God as I drove from the doctor's office that day, trying my best to wipe the tears from my eyes so they would not block my ability to see the road. I remember literally crying out to God saying, "Lord, how can this be? You told me I had something special to do. You told me I would achieve great things! I know I haven't been perfect. Yes, I've made some mistakes... BUT REALLY GOD! Why me? Why now? Have I failed you? Lord, have a failed you?"

Even in the midst of my confusion in that moment, in the midst of my pain and worry; even in the midst of me not knowing how much longer I would have to live, behind the tears... deep down within, as I drove from the hospital on that cold day in November, I felt God say: "My Child, Just Trust Me."

Soon after leaving the doctor's office, God immediately confirmed His command to just trust Him through my mother. She was the first person I told. She was the only one I could confide in at the time. I remember her reaction to the news. Honestly, I had braced myself fearing that when she received this information she would break down, terrified that her only daughter could soon die. But surprisingly enough, she did just the opposite. That's how strong her faith in God was.

In the quietness and stillness of our home basement, when I told my mother I had just received the news that I was HIV Positive, she looked at me, and then she smiled and said these exact words that I will never forget: "Ok Rhonda. Now let me ask you this: Is there anything too hard for God? I want you to remember Job in the Bible. He was tried; he too was tested. He too became sick, but no matter what, he still trusted God. Don't ever forget that. God's got you, you hear me! God's got you!"

As my mother embraced me, I felt an overwhelming sense of peace. At that moment, I knew God had used my mother to confirm to me that everything was going to be ok.

But I must admit, although the peace was present, so too was the confusion, the overwhelming fear, and the embarrassment; still, there was the regret and the uncertainty. At that moment, even though it had been confirmed that God was going to take care of me, I made a conscious choice.

In that moment, I still allowed my fears to set in. I allowed my fear of the future to override God's promises. I allowed the fear of what I firmly believed others would say or how I thought others would think of me to cancel out what God had already told me. I allowed the appearance of my current situation to override the ordained plan God had already made for my life. I allowed my mindset, my thoughts, my actions, my reality, and even my relationships, to be negatively affected by the ten-minute conversation I had with the doctor – the seven words the doctor gave me that cold day in November 2004.

Consequently, a deep-rooted chain of all these negative emotions began to link together that affected me for approximately the next five years of my life.

On the outside, I appeared well accomplished. I appeared great and successful. I ministered to many about having endless faith and walked around with a smile on my face. But, truth be told, on the inside, I suffered from fear, low self-esteem and a lack of faith myself. Because of this deep-rooted issue within me, I began to allow myself to engage in abusive relationships, both mentally and sometimes physically. I honestly didn't know if anyone would ever truly love me for me. Even though my exterior was beautiful and I had the support and confidence of my parents, deep down I had already written myself off when the whole time God was trying to tell me, "My Child, JUST TRUST ME!"

In the Bible, in Ecclesiastes 3:1 it states, "There is a time for everything, and a season for every action under heaven." As with the weather, seasons come and seasons go. At one point of my life I was living in a season of fear, worry and doubt; I was living in a season of being chained by my HIV Diagnosis. I'm proud today to say that this season of my life no longer exists. Yes, it took me a while to overcome this season, but, with faith, a conscious decision to believe God's promises, and truly learning to love all of me, that season has passed. There came a point in my life where I had to seriously take a look at myself. I had to start with the woman in the mirror.

After years of suffering inside and holding onto the chain of fear, I had to make the conscious decision to no longer walk around afraid, but live fully in faith; faith in what I knew God could do. Faith in what I preached to others about all the time. I had to make the conscious decision to believe Jesus at His word and stand steadfast on His promise. His promise in Jeremiah 29:11 that He has a plan to prosper me and not harm me, a plan to give me a hope and a future. The promise found in 1 Corinthians 10:13 that "God is faithful; he will not let you be tempted beyond what you can bear." The promise found in Romans 8:28 that "in *all* things God works for the good of those who love him, who have been called according to his purpose."

During this season of being hemmed up in chains, while I had honestly never been hospitalized, physically hurt, or physically hindered because of my HIV, I decided to let go and let God take control. That was when I truly began to experience the total inner manifestation of my healing.

See, so many times, we only see healing and deliverance from illness as a physical revelation, but the truth is this: One day, our fleshly exterior is going to diminish. It is going to die. True deliverance and true healing take place when one has a holistic peace within. When one doesn't allow their condition or their diagnosis to determine their mindset. I've learned over the years that complete and true healing goes beyond the doctor's words "You are healed!" For the truth is, according to the scriptures in Isaiah 53:5, "by his stripes, we are healed." Not "we may be healed" or "we will be healed." We *are* healed! For some of us, like myself, for so many years, God is waiting for us to transform our mindsets about what true healing means. Then, and only then, will we ultimately experience the level of deliverance, peace, and ultimate healing that we so desire and long for. For many of us, God is waiting on us to just trust Him at His Word. His word where He says He will never leave us or forsake us. His word that says that all things work for the good of those who love Him. All things! Not some things; not just good things; not 99.9% of things. All things! This means the good, bad, and the ugly! Know that in all of it, through any diagnosis, God can and will work it all out for your good.

As I look back over this season of my life, I realize now that being diagnosed with HIV was one of the best things that could have ever happened to me. "Why?" you may ask. Well, being diagnosed with HIV forced me to really rely on God and take Him at His word wholeheartedly. Having HIV has allowed me to be a living miracle for people to see that being diagnosed is not a death sentence. Rather, it's an opportunity for Christ to truly manifest His healing power in your life.

As I look back on November 2004 after I was told this life-changing, awakening news, I truly thought my life was over. Now, I truly get excited and simply smile because my life has proven to be a testament of how faithful God truly is! I smile as I embrace my three healthy, beautiful children. I thank God for providing me with a husband that loves every bit of me and my testimony. I look at the healing power of God as I think about the fact that, for years now, the HIV virus has been undetectable in my body. I am grateful when I think about the times doctors have looked at me in amazement, wondering how I am doing so well. All I could do was smile back at them and say: "It's because of Jesus."

I realize having HIV has been a remarkable blessing, because God saw fit to choose me; He saw fit to make a miracle out of me. He saw fit to make sure that, even in the midst of a diagnosis; I still experienced deliverance once I fully put my trust in Him.

Now, I have a fearless faith, an unwavering joy, an unending gratitude knowing that I must tell this story to let others who have been diagnosed with any illness know it's not over. Honestly, it's only just begun! Know that, if this is you, if you have been diagnosed with an illness, whether it be chronical, terminal, physical, or mental; know that your diagnosis is not a death sentence. Know that even in the midst of what you may be going through, God's word still stands true.

Know that, in the midst of a diagnosis, there are many things you can do to begin to tap into your own divine healing. First, you must be sure to not allow your condition to have you lose faith in the promises God has already set before you. Second, you must transform your thinking about what true healing means. To transform means to change. You must change your negative thoughts about what can happen or what may happen. Rather, you must focus your mind on the positive realities ahead of you. How life will be when you overcome. The lives you will impact through your story. Focus on how grateful you are to still have breath in your body right now. Third, you must see your deliverance beyond the physical realm. The truth is, whether you are diagnosed with an illness or not, if you live, your physical body will someday pass away. Know that, beyond your physical body, you have been gifted with eternal life by Jesus Christ. This, my friend, is forever. No diagnosis, disease, or ailment can take this away from you! Rejoice in this fact. Also, fourth, during this time, it is important to surround yourself with individuals who will support you and remind you of the fact that every breath is a blessing, regardless of your diagnosis. Do not waste them worrying about tomorrow, but use them to enhance your life, the lives of individuals around you, and become the vessel of greatness God has ordained you to become. Know that, with a diagnosis, your life has not ended! Truthfully, it has only just begun!

It is your responsibility, your mandate, to continue to push forth; put aside the chain of worry, fear, resentment, or depression, and push towards what God's intended for you. Understand, in the word testimony is the strong, but powerful four-letter word called test. Know that, sometimes, you must go through the test before you get to the testimony. But like me, your testimony will be strong, impact lives, and change the world.

Now, I am excited to say that, no longer am I bound and chained by fear. No longer am I concerned about what others think or what they may say. At the age of five, during a revival service I went to with my grandmother in my hometown church, God told me He was going to use me to reach the masses. I remember that day so vividly. Being a young girl at the time, while I didn't fully understand what that meant when I felt and heard God on that day, now I know. Now, years later, I understand being diagnosed with HIV and in return, being healed and delivered, is a part of my purpose and my story. It is a part of my ministry. God has allowed me to connect with women across the world through my international ministry to offer hope and provide deliverance to them in the midst of their own diagnosis.

If you have been diagnosed with a condition and would like support if you can relate to my story and would like to connect; if you are living your life in fear, worry, shame, or depression because of a positive test result from any diagnosis, know that Rhonda Watts-Robinson International Ministries is here to support you, encourage you, pray with you, and guide you along the way. You don't have to walk this walk alone. It doesn't matter if it's HIV or AIDS; it doesn't matter if it's cancer, depression, diabetes, fibromyalgia, lupus, etc. Whatever the diagnosis, know you are delivered! Know your healing awaits you! I invite you to take the first step on your journey of deliverance and healing by downloading the FREE Divine Healing Handbook at www.DivineHealingHandbook.com. Within this powerful healing handbook, you will be provided with thirty-one days of healing scriptures, prayers, reflections, and affirmations to assist you in manifesting your healing and deliverance. God has promised in His word, in Isaiah 53:5, "by his stripes we are healed."

Through The Divine Healing Handbook, you will be led and guided through thirty-one life changing days of short readings that will assist you in tapping into your divine healing; the healing that is already given to you!

Your Illness Does Not Define You

Your Strength and

Courage Does

-Unknown

My hope for you, my friend, is that, today, you will walk away from reading my story and know that it's not your illness or your diagnosis that matters. It's your strength, your courage; it's your faith and fearlessness; it's your conscious decision to focus forward and not stay stuck in worry and fear. This is my hope for you today. It is my challenge for you to let the remainder of your days, the remainder of your breaths be full of gratefulness and unwavering faith in the fact that all things work together for the good of those who love God. Know your healing and your holistic deliverance is much closer than you think. Let today be the day you embrace it and live each moment to the fullest!

No More Fear:

I don't want to talk about fear, because I know that fear is something we create, so that means it's something we have the power to let go. As I've read Rhonda's story over and over again, I feel compelled to speak about change. Change is what we go through when we release our fears.

So many of us sit on the verge of change. Change requires letting go of fear and shame as Rhonda had to face, which catapulted her into her new. Her new space. Her new calling. Her new ministry. I feel a need to send you a reminder today to love yourself deeply through this process.

+ As you let something go, don't judge yourself for holding onto it for too long. Instead, love yourself for finding the courage to finally release it.

+ As you start making changes, don't criticize yourself for the place you find "yourself" now. Instead, honor yourself for your courage to face it and transform it.

+ As you step into the new, don't be hard on yourself if you make mistakes. Be proud of the trust and strength you are showing to be willing to face the unknown.

Change is hard. Growth is uncomfortable. So what your precious self needs now isn't more judgment, criticism or doubt. It needs love. Love, support, encouragement, and patience.

So love yourself a little more right now. Drop the shame, guilt, judgment, and regret.

Breathe into your belly and then breathe all that crap out.

And be grateful for this moment now, as this is your moment to create something brand new.

This moment now is your clean slate. ~Ari Squires

Affirm this: I am willing to let this go. I welcome in the new.

About Tiffanye S. Wesley

Tiffanye S. Wesley is a Fire/EMS Captain II with the Arlington County Fire Department, Arlington, VA. She is the first African American female to be promoted in the department's 71-year history. In her 23 years of service, she has served in numerous positions within the department. The two most notable positions were becoming a Nationally Certified Bomb Technician and Bomb Commander and most recently becoming the Station Commander for the largest and busiest firehouse in Arlington.

Tiffanye recently decided to invest in her lifelong dream of becoming an Inspirational Speaker, Author and Trainer. She has been aggressive in her goals and by April of 2017 she will have obtained all three. She was recently featured in a short video on You Tube titled, "Breaking the glass ceiling" by a Georgetown University graduate student. Tiffanye was also recently selected to be a presenter at the largest Fire Department Instructor's Conference (FDIC) which last year had more than 39, 000 attendees. Tiffanye will also be featured in a book anthology with the "Big Money Speaker" James Malinchak, titled *Reach YOUR Greatness, Top Thought-Leaders Share Their Secrets for Living an Extraordinary Life!*

Tiffanye has been an inspiration to women all over the Country just by being transparent and sharing her story of determination and commitment in a career that no one ever thought she would survive in. Her 'No Matter What 'and 'If they say I can't, I will prove that I can' attitude has allowed her to climb the ladder of success even when the odds were stacked against her. Tiffanye uses prayer, poetry and positive affirmations daily to keep her focused and renewed. She also commits to a healthy lifestyle of eating and exercise.

Tiffanye is married to her best friend Eric Wesley, who is also a firefighter in Arlington County. They have four beautiful children and 1 grandchild.

Chapter 11

I'm Anointed for this!

TIFFANYE S. WESLEY

–⦿⦿⦿⦿⦿⦿⦿–

My stomach is queasy and my mind is playing tricks
I refuse to give up now because I know I'm anointed for this
I'm feeling overwhelmed and my heart is starting to flutter
I am determined to press on because I know it's to bless another
You may wonder how I continue to fight with a smile on my face
You may even wonder how I was able to pay for a 4-year long case
Well, I'm not afraid to share my story to give you a glimpse of hope
My account is overdrawn, all my bills are late and I am literally broke
I can't pay my mortgage, my attorney or my daycare
There are days when I scream out, "God this isn't fair!"
Fair or not I get up, dressed in the 'whole armor' and peace on my lips
I believe in my calling, "I'm anointed for this!"
I will continue to put my trust in God, who sits high and looks low
He will never leave me nor forsake me, his word tells me so
And while some may still wonder why I took on such a huge risk
Why I continued despite a pending foreclosure and after my case was dismissed
Well, I will tell you a few things I've learned along the way
These virtues that I've learned still hold true to this very day
The race is the hardest at the very end
And without test, trials and endurance, it's impossible to win

God is the same God as he was yesterday, today and forever more

It doesn't matter what happens in life nor does it matter who's keeping score

So as I prepare to walk into court and as I approach the bench with clenched fist

Win, lose or draw I declare, "I'm anointed for this!"

Wow! I still remember the day I wrote this poem as if it were yesterday. See, this poem was written on September 29, 2009, days before I was set to walk into Circuit Court for a 3-day discrimination lawsuit against my employer. I was broke and broken at the time but I refused to give up. I knew deep down inside that one day my story would inspire someone to keep going. I knew I had a calling in my life years prior to this experience. See, I grew up in church and I even went to a Christian school but it wasn't until I began to experience "life" on my own that I truly began to get it.

Life – as I saw it growing up – was all about doing well in school so I could go to college, graduate from college, get a good paying job, get married, have a family and live happily ever after. I grew up in a loving two-parent household with an older brother and sister. My parents took us to church every Sunday and I remember before breakfast on Sundays we had to go around the table and recite a scripture. It didn't matter if it were the same scripture from week to week, you just better have one to recite. I think back on those days with a huge smile on my face. I smile because that is my foundation. My foundation was a solid one built on love and respect in the home. It was a foundation that was further solidified when my mother took me out of public school in the 7th grade and sent me to Christian school. Of course, at the time, I was not happy but looking back now, I appreciate all of the scriptures I had to memorize every week. The same scriptures I remember and rely on to this day. I appreciate the teachers that instilled in us through non-traditional teaching that we were "More than Conquerors". We learned to affirm who we were before affirmations were popular. I believe that is why I love affirmations to this day. I not only love creating them but I love sharing and helping others create them for themselves. It is also the reason I have decided to share a 7-day affirmation and poetry journal with everyone who reads my story. The 7-day journal will give you a hope and a future.

My story is one of just that, a hope and a future. I began my career and my fight in the Fire Service in 1994. I heard an announcement on WHUR radio looking for men AND women to join a team of professionals helping people in the community…saving lives. The word that stood out to me most was CAREER. See, my plans had already been altered, well should I say the plans my parents had for my life had already been altered. My parents preached for 12 years, "Go to school, get a good education and leave those boys alone!" Well, like most teenagers, I was hardheaded. I went to school, got accepted into college and even got accepted into a prestigious internship at Disney World my first year in college. It sounds good except for the part where I eloped the week prior to leaving for my internship at Disney. The story gets even better. A year later I found out I was pregnant and I was forced to confess that I was already married. My parents' plans and dreams for me were now shattered and now I was forced to find a CAREER. The announcement on the radio sounded appealing enough, even though I didn't know any firefighters male or female. I had never been to a firehouse or even interacted with a firefighter. None of those things mattered to me; all I heard was the word career. I applied and a few days later, I drove the hour to take the physical agility test and I failed. This was the first failure. In total, I took the physical agility three times before I was able to pass it. It was somewhere between the second and third time trying that I discovered that I had to get serious. See, the attitude of "let me try this" was not going to work in this situation. The attitude and sentiment is what I pass on to ladies today who have a desire to join the Fire Service. It takes hard work and determination to be successful.

I carried that mindset of hard work and determination into the fire recruit school. I had to! As soon as I realized the physical agility was not the only test that I would have to pass. I soon learned that some of the test and obstacles were not meant for me to pass. I learned that some of the people in the Fire Service did not believe I should even be there.

My first fight came a week prior to graduating from recruit school. This particular agency had a '3 strike you out rule' meaning if you fail something three times you are dismissed (fired). It didn't matter if it was three different things you failed or if it were a week prior to graduation. Well, they said I failed an evolution of repelling from a building and lowering someone with a hasty hitch. The union fought on my behalf because it was something that had never been done in real life. It was a question if I really failed because I did get my victim to the ground safely on a repel rope.

Nonetheless, I was fired and I was devastated! My parents still had my celebratory cookout that was planned with family and friends. I told everyone that weekend that I was going to apply to another agency. See, I was met with so much negativity in the beginning that I refused to give up. I heard everything from, "you are too small" to "it's an all white male profession"to "they will never accept you". The more opposition I had and the more negativity, the more I wanted to do it even more. I affirmed that day that 'No Matter What' I would succeed in the Fire Service.

Four short months later, I sat in another jurisdiction, in another fire recruit school. This was nothing but God's work because the hiring process alone normally took 6-9 months. I started this recruit school with a confidence no one would believe. I was 5'2 and 115 lbs. soaking wet but I had a made-up mind. I was determined to finish what I had started. I had something to prove to all of my nay- sayers and I certainly had something to prove to the agency that fired me.

I passed recruit school 22 weeks later and I was excited! I was sent to a fire station with an African-American Captain. The Captain, whom I still to this day call my second daddy, not only protected me but he also instilled in me the knowledge and confidence that I needed to be successful. I was teased coming into the firehouse but I had an older brother so I could handle it. I was embraced by my crew and welcomed to the family as it is often referred to. I thought I was 'all good!'

I was 'all good' in my career, until I decided I wanted more than to ride on the back step of a fire truck. I wanted to be more than a firefighter; I wanted to be an officer. I first attempted to become a paramedic but was unsuccessful at the end of the school but I refused to let that stop me. I began to understand that what doesn't kill you makes you stronger, especially in the fire service. I later began to sit for promotional exams. My very first captain exam in 2003, I came out in the top list and was eligible to be promoted. I didn't get promoted that year but I chalked it up as, "I'm still new, it wasn't my time" See, these types of attitudes are engraved into your mind early in your career.

Two years later, I sat for another captain promotional exam but again I was not promoted. Around the same time, I also applied to the Fire Prevention Office but was unsuccessful. It was 2005 and I was fed up with "the system" so I filed a grievance. I later would have to file downtown at the Washington, DC Equal Employment

Office. Two years later, I sat for a 3rd promotional exam but this time, Lieutenants had been added back into our rank structure. While waiting on my filing to be investigated, I was promoted to Lieutenant. This promotion marked the first time an African-American female had been promoted in the department's 71-year history. I was proud but still not ready to back down from a fight I started 2 years prior. One week from my promotion, I received a letter from EEOC granting me a right to sue. After meeting with the Fire Chief and not being able to come up with a viable solution, I hired an attorney. As I stated earlier, what doesn't kill you makes you stronger.

I got stronger and stronger over the next 2 years of my fight. I literally went broke fighting my case but I did not give up! I refused to give up! Even after my case was dismissed, I hired another attorney to fight the appeal. I won the appeal, which led to a 3-day trial. Unfortunately, I did not win! I tell people all the time, "I lost but I won!" I won a confidence you would never believe. My faith grew even stronger, many days crying out to God to just keep my mind. I continued to go to work every day with a smile on my face. The smile I believe helped me to gain the respect I still have today. Many to this day do not know my story. Many do not know what I had to go through. I still have not shared everything in this short chapter. There were many poems and affirmations born out of this experience. My poems and affirmations that I am sharing through this book anthology and my 7-day mindset makeover are meant to inspire and give you a desire to want more in life just as I did in my fight to get to where I am today.

See, I knew this day would come. The day where I would be able to share my story and bless another female. I pray for the one reading this story right now, no matter what profession or stage in life you are in. I pray you will begin to release the chains of devastation and embarrassment as I once held. I pray the chains of giving up, the chains of defeat, the chains of despair, the chains of feeling not smart enough, or strong enough will all be broken by the time you finish reading this book.

You see, we all know what failure looks and feels like. We have all survived something in life that at the time we thought we would never have been able to survive. One of my favorite quotes says, "It's not how you start but how you finish." That is the mindset I began to adopt in my most challenging times. I knew there would be a day when no one would even remember the test that I took in

2003 or 2005 and did not get promoted. The way I am finishing is what's important and what will be remembered long after I retire.

You have to develop a belief system, one that makes you the most important building block in that system. Once you start believing in yourself just as I did, you will begin to have confidence in your own abilities. No one will be able to define or label you. You will release the chains because you know who you are! You will understand what it means to succeed against the odds because you have already done it! You will begin to understand what Eleanor Roosevelt meant in yet another one of my favorite quotes, "No one can make you feel inferior without your consent"

I am often asked how I did it? How I survived all of these years? How did I manage to break the glass ceiling? This is the part of my story that I most enjoy sharing. I started with a mindset makeover! I began to see the end in the beginning. I began to read and study my craft more so I would never be caught off guard. I began to create powerful affirmations and repeat them daily. I began to follow the principles of success, the same ones I will share in my 7-day free mindset makeover. Most importantly, I began each day on purpose. I committed to a life of prayer, positive affirmations and powerful success principles.

Through this lifestyle, I am happy to announce that I stand as a Captain II and Station Commander of the busiest firehouse in my department. I am also proud to say that I survived 23 years and I am now preparing to become the First African-American Female Battalion Chief in my department. Although I am still the only promoted African-American female in my department, I have made the commitment to not be the last. I also commit to helping other women like myself release the chains and continue to fight for what they believe in and what they deserve because just as the poem I wrote 7 years ago, "I'm anointed for this!"

No More Settling:

What I love about Tiffanye's story is that it is not one of a devastating negative life trauma. She had loving parents, who cared for her and raised her with good morals and to follow her heart, not her head. Her story is one to encourage us to see how a strong family dynamic can set future generations up for success; mentally, emotionally and spiritually. Her parents taught her how to fight and have strong faith by instilling a positive environment.

My question is, what examples will you continue to make to the children in your life? Children need good examples so they know that if ever faced with the obstacles Tiffanye faced, they too can succeed. That took a strong foundation.

Write a thank you letter to yourself for what you do that is positive in a child's life, that encourages them to be all they can be. Sometimes we have to take a moment and pat ourselves on the back and praise ourselves for the positive things we do.

Kudos to Tiffanye for breaking the chains in career and giving women hope for what's possible for them. ~Ari Squires

Write your thank you letter to yourself for all that you do to be the best example you can be.

_____

_____

_____

_____

_____

_____

_____

_____

_____

_____

    I found it very prevalent that Tiffanye lives from her heart. This is where all possibility lives. She follows her heart in all the things she does.

    What is your heart calling you towards?

    I want you to imagine your heart can talk to you. It communicates to you through the feeling of love. When you feel that you would love to do something that is your heart telling you it is right for you.

What is one thing your heart has been calling you to do, but your head is telling you that you can't do?

_____

_____

_____

_____

_____

List all of the reasons why you would love to do it:

_____

_____

_____

_____

_____

_____

_____

_____

_____

_____

What crappy stories has your fearful mind been telling you which has been stopping you from following your heart?

_____

_____

_____

_____

_____

Are you ready to let these go?

_____

_____

_____

_____

What is the worst thing that could happen if you decide to follow your heart?

_____

_____

_____

_____

Can you make peace with that?

_____

_____

_____

_____

_____

At this point, I want you to decide which voice you are going to listen to. If you choose to listen to your head, there is no need to continue with this exercise. If you choose to follow your heart, then please continue.

What risk are you willing to take in order to follow your heart?

_____

_____

_____

_____

_____

What will you have to let go of (mentally, emotionally or physically) in order to follow your heart?

_____

_____

_____

_____

_____

If you are ready to follow through and really follow your heart, please declare your commitment below.

I have decided to follow my heart, no matter what, and so I declare that I am going to:

_____

_____

_____

_____

_____

Write a love note from your inner cheerleader to give yourself some loving support about all of the reasons why you can do this.

_____

_____

_____

_____

_____

_____

_____

_____

_____

What is the very first step you are going to take?

_____

_____

_____

_____

When are you going to take this step?

_____

_____

_____

_____

_____

Go to the Facebook group "Release The Chains Business Empowerment Group" and declare your step along with the hashtag #NoMoreChains and the date that you are going to complete it by.

We are all going to hold you accountable!

Afterword

What it Means to Be Free

ABIOLA ABRAMS

Releasing the chains that bind is far from easy. We all grew up hearing adults tell us to love ourselves, but we didn't know what that meant. Most of the time, they didn't know what that meant either. With all of the turmoil and strife that we face, this is a gift that we have that no generation who came before us ever had. Things are far from perfect, but we have the possibility to really be able to create a sense of freedom in our lives, whatever that means to you.

I am what Donald Trump and company have called an "anchor baby." When I was born, my mother was an undocumented immigrant. She came to America with $20 in her pocket. She cried when she arrived and saw how dirty New York City was because it didn't look like the movies she had watched in her country. Although she and my dad come from the same small village in Guyana, South America, they met in Brooklyn. It was the 1970s. Afros were popping and so was politics. I guess it was kind of like this moment right now.

My parents were both raised by farmers. Their parents didn't have time to talk about loving yourself. My mom's dad only went up to the 6th grade, but somehow became the councilman of his village. My dad's dad knew he wanted better for his son and urged my dad to pursue "book work" instead of farming.

Most of our great-grands and grandparents never contemplated that all things were possible for them. Many of us grew up with that idea already in the ether, even if it wasn't in our households. In that way we are privileged. We have to acknowledge that. Let's not take that privilege that was born on the backs of very hard working and often oppressed and silenced people and bury it.

When our neighbors who looked just like us beat up my family and told us to go back to our country, I couldn't complain to my mom. Somehow, I knew that she had seen much worse. I knew that she was sacrificing to make a better life for me. I knew even as a kid that if I could release my own chains, I would be freeing generations past and future as well.

When my mother borrowed my flashcards to make her own to study for her American citizenship exam, I knew then that freedom ain't free. We have to work for it – with everything we have. By hard work I am not just talking about sweat equity and hours accrued, I am talking about the inner work that will stop us from sabotaging ourselves. I am talking about getting out of your own way so that you can step into your greatness. I'm talking about making the calls, showing up for the meetings, being a leader and putting yourself out there.

In this book you have read the lessons of brilliant women who have overcome tremendous adversity. Usually when we think of success, we just see the end game. Hopefully, you don't just admire what they have been able to do, but you take these lessons to release the chains in your own life.

Each of us has a story to tell. Everyone one of us has overcome something seemingly insurmountable. You have that in common with Ari Squires and with me. You also have that in common with Oprah Winfrey, Maya Angelou, Barack Obama and Muhammed Ali.

We don't get to choose what life throws at us, but we do get to choose how we deal with it. Being bullied on a daily basis led in part to me developing extreme issues with anxiety. People ask how I can be on stages around the country or on TV worldwide and say that I have social anxiety. The answer is that my purpose is bigger than my problems. I am needed on TV giving advice so that a little girl somewhere who looks like me has one less excuse.

Do you think that if either one of my grandfathers had social anxiety they could take a week off from the farm? I have to step up because I was called and I am answering that calling. I am urging you to do the same. You are needed on the front. There is important work that you were born to do.

Self-determination, self-love, and self-worth don't come bundled with the degree. The strength to keep going another day when things seem impossible are not attached to the certification. The will to keep going can only come from you.

When you feel like quitting, remember why you started in the first place. When you want to give up, think about whether you will be cheating others by retreating. Now, I'm not saying that you shouldn't make a U-Turn. The road to freedom and answering your calling will be filled with U-Turns. Any success has also had a ton of failures. What I am saying is don't take the failures as a period; see them as a comma and keep moving forward.

No matter who you are and what your story is, someone from your past paid for your future. Step up to the plate. You know how they say that we are the ones we've been waiting for? It's true. The reason you keep thinking that folks are stealing your ideas is that you're not stepping up. God gives us the ideas for what is needed in the world. If you don't do it then someone else is called forward.

Stop asking people who don't even believe in themselves to believe in you. Believe in yourself.

Each of us holds a piece of the sacred puzzle to make a corner of the world a better place. What are you going to do with yours?

Release the chains and move forward. I'll see you on the
frontlines. -Abiola Abrams
Award-winning Author, Speaker, Coach, Founder of
ManifestYourPower.com

ACKNOWLEDGEMENTS

Through my journey, there have been so many people who have stood by me, held my hand, lent their shoulder, mentored me and impacted my life. It's impossible to acknowledge everyone so please accept my apology if you were missed. Please know that I appreciate and love you with all my heart.

Acknowledgements not listed in any particular order.

First and foremost I have to give thanks to my creator who helps me tap into my power every day and keeps me grounded in love and gratitude. Special gratitude must go to: My mother, Sherman Heidelberg, Addie Heidelberg, Marjorie Lawson, Jermone Thrower, Tia Terry, Keshia & Kaila Redmond, Tiffany Griffith, Andre Henley, Vicki Irvin, Zenovia & Anthony Andrews, James Malinchak, Tony Gaskins, Vikki Johnson, Vicki Saunders, Charlotte Avery, Lisa Nichols, Steve Harvey, Kevin Hart, Allyson Byrd, Haki Ammi, George C. Fraser, Theresa Royal Brown, Joan Wilson, Jasper White, Paul C. Brunson, Patrice C. Washington, Darrin Henson, Abiola Abrams, Joy Pearson, Julie Roane, Treneze and Bobby Lacy, Delvelyn Pruitt, Pastor Timothy Jackson, Craig Boothe, Patricia Clement, Leslie Jackson, Nanyamka Payne, Felicia Fuller, Taliah Shiree Graves, Latoya Johnson, Thomas Osam Jr., Lisa Layton-Mehr, Ginger Miller, Andre Henley, Common, Oprah Winfrey, Iyanla Vanzant, Nat Turner, Malcolm X, Dr. Venus Opal Reese, Shanel Cooper-Sykes, Zakiya Larry, Alysia Lacy, Tony Robbins, Jonathan Sprinkles, David Banner, Les Brown, Roland Martin, Kali Mystic Rose, Paul Robeson, WEB Du Bois, Marcus Garvey, Martin Luther King Jr., Tony Browder, Napoleon Hill, Alain Locke, Una Marson, Kwame Nkrumah, 2Pac, Mary J. Blige, Beyonce', Jay-Z, Mimi G. Style, Tiffany Aliche, Cheryl Wood, Lucinda Cross, Erykah Badu, Aye Waiter, Robyn Gray, Charita Mariner, Anthony Poole, Taraji P. Henson, Panache Desai, Belinda Davidson, Chereace & Stan Richards, Ice Cube, Spike Lee, Robert Townsend, Keenan

Ivory Wayans, Bill Cosby, Richard Pryor, Sabir Bey, Dr. Umar Johnson, Tariq Nasheed, John Henrick Clarke, Chantelle Cotton, Black Enterprise Magazine, Essence Magazine, Sophia Nelson, Maricia Sherman, Brian Heat, Ebro Darden, Ashley Johnson, Walter Dawson, Mayasa Telfair, Ebony Moss, Reggie Sanders, Tyler Perry, John Singleton, Patrick Cave & Family, Rialand Jones, Chiezda Washington, Mike Fonenot, Kimberly Arrington, Gary Holland, Angie Smith, James Jackson & TopKats, Jackie Jackson, Crystal Jones, Ozzy Ramos, Niambi Rockcliffe, Gregory Turner, Cynthia Dixon, Sydney & Shondella Murray, Ray Pope, Chesa Richmond, Lois Powell, Reverend Earnest Woodson III, Teal Gregory, Nyea Corbin, Mats Jerndall, Mayeisha Parker, Denia Weaver, Gabe Beau, Sheila Snipes, Tyrese, K. Michelle, Tee Marie, Quniana Futrell, Amanda Eaddy Oliver, Theresa Alexis, Erica Hill, Terecita Sterling, Rhonda Watts-Robinson, Tiffanye S. Wesley. And so many other people who have helped me get through some storms, given me a shot, or have inspired me to be greater...whether they know it or not!

SPECIAL ACKNOWLEDGEMENT

Special acknowledgement to my husband Darryl Squires, who puts up with me and all my crazy ideas. He tells me the truth even if I don't want to hear it or expect it, and trusts me enough to let me go after my dreams with no restrictions, disempowerment or chains. I promise, I will retire you one day soon. I owe you my life! My nine-year-old son, my ride-or-die, and business-partner Amare M. Squires (King-Boss), you are my rock. Without you, nothing I do would be meaningful or possible. I appreciate your reminders, help and encouragement. You sure do keep mommy on her toes. You will make a great business man one day. If nobody else has my back, I know you will. My daughter, Avanti Squires for forcing me to be the best example and role model I can be and sharing you random kinds words of love and support. I thank you three for being my light, joy and covering.

NO MORE CHAINS

"You Can Do Anything"

ARI SQUIRES, MISS SHEEO
BUSINESS STRATEGIST & AUTHENTIC LIFESTYLE COACH

THE
FREEDOM
MOVEMENT
CHALLENGE FOR VISIONARIES

#NoMoreChains

A FREE Program Teaching Visionaries how to Release Their Chains and learn the Power of Story$elling: Building a Business Around Your Unique Story and Impacting Lives!

Join The Challenge NOW!

WWW.MYSTORYHASPURPOSE.COM

www.ingramcontent.com/pod-product-compliance
Lightning Source LLC
Chambersburg PA
CBHW072011090426

42740CB00011B/2152